"Dads set the tone for their families. Really good dads make a significant difference in their families and their neighborhoods. Rick Johnson shows you ten things good dads do. If you want to strengthen your family and prepare your children to succeed in life, this book shows you how."

—**Pat Williams**, author of *It's Not Who You Know, It's Who You Are*

"Every dad I know desires to be a great father, but they don't always know where to begin. If that describes you, I encourage you to start with Rick's new book, *10 Things Great Dads Do*! Rick's books have always been the place I go to for practical wisdom and insight into how to be a better dad. *Better Dads, Stronger Sons* has helped me in the raising of my two boys, and *Becoming the Dad Your Daughter Needs* has been a great encouragement as I raise my three girls. I'm excited to have this latest book—it will impact me as a father to all of my children. Reading this book is a great step to growing a stronger family."

—**Rob Teigen**, bestselling author of *88 Great Daddy-Daughter Dates*

"Better than anyone I know, Rick Johnson presents relational philosophies that make sense. And then: *Bam!* Before you know it he has given you real-life ways to apply what you just read. Invest a few bucks and a couple hours in *10 Things Great Dads Do* and you'll instantly know the 'whys' and the 'hows' of fantastic fathering."

—**Jay Payleitner**, conference speaker and bestselling author of *52 Things Kids Need from a Dad* and *The Dad Book*

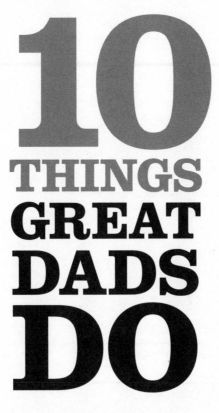

10 THINGS GREAT DADS DO

STRATEGIES FOR RAISING GREAT KIDS

RICK JOHNSON

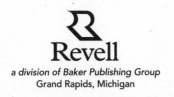

Revell
a division of Baker Publishing Group
Grand Rapids, Michigan

Published by Revell
a division of Baker Publishing Group
P.O. Box 6287, Grand Rapids, MI 49516-6287
www.revellbooks.com

Printed in the United States of America

Library of Congress Cataloging-in-Publication Data
Johnson, Rick, 1956–
10 things great dads do : strategies for raising great kids / Rick Johnson.
pages cm
Includes bibliographical references.
ISBN 978-0-8007-2235-7 (pbk.)
1. Fatherhood—Religious aspects—Christianity. 2. Parenting—Religious aspects—Christianity. 3. Child rearing—Religious aspects—Christianity. 4. Fathers—Religious life. I. Title. II. Title: Ten things great dads do.
BV4529.17.J63 2015
248.8′421—dc23 2015016517

The author is represented by WordServe Literary Group.

15 16 17 18 19 20 21 7 6 5 4 3 2 1

I dedicate this book to all the grandfathers out there who have stepped up and are parenting their grandchildren. You have a much tougher road than anyone knows. But without your presence, so many more children would fall through the cracks of life.

May God bless you
and give you the strength to persevere!
You truly are Better Dads.

Contents

Acknowledgments

As is often the case, the people who really deserve much of the credit for a book seldom get the credit they are due. I've tried to mention all the people at my publisher who deserve credit in past books and failed miserably. So let me just thank and acknowledge *everyone* who works at Revell and Baker Publishing Group. A finer group of people to work with I've never met. I'm honored to have worked with all of you for the past nine years or so.

I'd also like to thank a few men who spoke some real wisdom to me while writing this book. Those men include Scott, Terry, Kenny, Darrel, and Stuart. Having friends like you guys makes me happier than getting a free pass to an all-you-can-eat pizza buffet at a ZZ Top concert. Well . . . almost.

Adversity toughens manhood, and the characteristic of the good or the great man is not that he has been exempt from the evils of life, but that he has surmounted them.

—Patrick Henry

In this life-long fight, to be waged by every one of us single-handed against a host of foes, the last requisite for a good fight, the last proof and test of our courage and manliness, must be *loyalty to truth*—the most rare and difficult of all human qualities. For such loyalty, as it grows in perfection, asks ever more and more of us, and sets before us a standard of manliness always rising higher and higher.

—Thomas Hughes, *The Manliness of Christ* (italics added)

I am the tallest oak now, exposed and vulnerable. And I'm increasingly suspicious of people. . . . All this started when I became a father, a faithful guardian of two innocent souls. And it grew worse when I lost my dad, and I realized there was no longer anyone I could run to. This is the evolution of man—from one who reaches out for comfort to one who is reached out to.

—Joe Kita, *The Father's Guide to the Meaning of Life*

In 1988 evangelical philosopher and theologian Carl Henry made a stunning prediction in his book, *Twilight of a Great Civilization* (Crossway Books). He said that as America progressively loses its Judeo-Christian heritage, paganism would grow bolder. What we saw in the last half of the 20th-century was a kind of benign humanism, but he predicted that by the start of the 21st-century, we would face a situation not unlike the first-century when the Christian faith confronted raw paganism—humanism with the pretty face ripped off, revealing the angry monster underneath. His words have come true, and are coming truer with every passing day.

—Dr. Ray Prichard

Introduction

The Bottom Line

All great dads have certain qualities that distinguish them from poor or even average fathers. Because they have these qualities, these dads give their kids a huge advantage in life. Their kids tend to be happier, healthier, and more successful in life than kids raised without these advantages. Not only that, the dads themselves garner more satisfaction out of their roles as fathers.

Of course, it's easy to *talk* about being a great dad—a better dad than we are now. But when the rubber meets the road, it's not always so easy to *be* a great dad. If we didn't have those qualities modeled for us by a father, it makes it even more difficult. Interestingly enough though, the qualities that make a great dad are easily learned and mastered by all men.

Most men *want* to be a better dad, even a great dad, but just don't know how. The problem is that many men don't know about these qualities—we are seldom trained in them unless we are fortunate enough to observe them from a wise, healthy male role model while growing up or have a group of men who mentor and intentionally teach us the importance of these qualities as boys. However, once we understand what our families need and want from us, becoming a better dad is a lot easier. That's what this book is about.

That doesn't mean that any of us will ever be a perfect dad, just that we don't quit trying to become a *better* dad. Certainly, I've never considered myself a great dad, but one area I couldn't be faulted in was lack of trying. Even my kids have to admit I was a better dad as they got older than I was when they were young. Part of that might be attributed to maturity on my part, or experience, but certainly most of it was due to a conscious effort to learn and grow as a father. That would seem obvious to most men, and yet I've known countless fathers who somehow seemed to give up or quit along the way. By the time their kids were grown, those kids either despised their dads or were oblivious to his presence.

I've studied, interviewed, counseled, and surveyed thousands of fathers over the past thirteen years as part of the work I do with families. Prior to that, I studied men who I thought were good fathers because I wanted to understand what a good father looked like. Having been raised in an alcoholic home, I understood what I *didn't* want to be like as a father, but I had no idea what kind of qualities I *should* have in order to be an effective father. Knowing what you don't want to be like as a father doesn't help much with how you should be as a father. Just doing the opposite of what you don't want to be like doesn't help either. I knew I didn't want to be a dad who hit my kids, but that didn't help me know how I should treat them instead.

This book looks at some of the unique characteristics or uncommon qualities that highly effective fathers possess. These behaviors turn average dads into great dads. Use these to go with the foundational attributes I discuss in some of my other fathering books, such as *Better Dads, Stronger Sons* and *Becoming the Dad Your Daughter Needs*. Those books are a kind of primer on what healthy fathering looks like as well as understanding your sons' and daughters' unique needs.

One way to determine what qualities we want to cultivate as a father is to start by taking some time alone (and then with your wife) to envision what kind of family you want to have. What kind of traits do you want to instill in your children? What values are most important to your family? What is the tone of your home going to be like? In my experience, those kinds of things do not just happen without some planning and then intentionality in making them come to fruition. For instance, you can't simply say, "I want to raise kids of character." There are dozens of character traits. Likely you won't be able to instill all those traits in your children no matter how great a father you are. But you can instill three or four key character traits by being aware of them and then being intentional about it. And of course we instill certain traits in our children just by modeling those traits. That's another reason for taking the time to plan what kind of family you want—it allows us to recognize what qualities we need to develop within ourselves in order to model them for our children. That way, regardless of what life throws at us, we have a game plan to fall back on. It also gives us a foundation to measure our progress against.

The truth is, dads matter. And good dads *really* matter. We are discovering after several decades of research that fathers play a very important role within the family and in the development of their children. In virtually every category that can be measured to determine success in life, children with involved fathers score significantly higher than children without fathers in their lives. Even biologically unrelated positive father figures make a difference.

An acquaintance of mine was talking about the importance of my book for fathers and daughters, *Becoming the Dad Your Daughter Needs*. She recounted the following story on the influence her husband had in a young girl's life:

> One of my daughters-in-law, whom we have known since she was 13, lost her father at age 5. My husband became her "Dad" in her early teens. Her sister had no such "stand-in." Looking at the lives of these two girls and how different they are is amazing. She is convinced her "dad" made the difference. I'd have to agree. He even walked her down the aisle when she married our son.

As a father you have been given the power to impact not only the lives of your own children but other children as well. Having power that we can use for good also means that power can be used negatively if abused or ignored. It's an awesome power that needs to be understood and used responsibly.

Being a father is hard. It may be the most difficult thing I've ever done (besides being a husband—which if not more difficult is certainly trickier). And it doesn't seem to get any easier. The older my kids get, the more difficult and complicated the issues seem to be (sorry, you guys with young children). My experiences with one child seldom seem relevant to the next child. And what works well in one situation rarely applies to the next.

But all things that are truly meaningful and significant in life are hard. And the more significant they are, the more difficult they become. So it goes without saying that if fathering is the most difficult thing you've ever done, it's probably because it's the most important and significant role you'll ever have. Certainly as a father you are indispensable and irreplaceable in the lives of your children in ways that are unimaginable.

Here's the good news. Fathering may be difficult, but it's also the most rewarding thing you will ever do. Billions of men throughout history have navigated fatherhood—some more successfully than others—but nearly all were able to do it if they chose to. So that means you can too! Since it's so important, your goal should be to do it as best as possible—you do that in every other area of your life, right? You are, as a matter of routine, the best employee you can be, the best softball player you can be, the best gamer, the best husband, and so on. Why not be the best father you can be as well? Perhaps because men seldom get kudos or public recognition for their fathering accomplishments, we tend not to be as intentional about our performance as we are in other areas of life.

Fatherhood is a cross-country marathon with plenty of obstacles along the way. It often requires us to engage in sprints or even sprints over hurdles. Just about the time we think we've figured out the course, some trap blindsides us and knocks us on our keister. If we don't find effective ways to deal with those challenges, it can turn us into frustrated and bitter men or defeated quitters. Unfortunately, quitting at fathering is not an option. It has huge negative ramifications in the lives of our children.

Being a grandfather has given me a whole new perspective on fathering. Without the stress and pressure of the financial responsibility of raising a family and a father's perceived obligation of being accountable for how my children turn out, I am able to sit back as a grandfather and view things a bit more objectively. I can see the bigger picture, if you will. From this perspective it's easier to see just how incredibly amazing and resilient children are. The ability to learn from scratch how to walk, speak a language (or several), become potty trained, and accumulate a vast sea of knowledge all in a few short years are some of the most stunning accomplishments on earth. We tend to take those accomplishments for granted because pretty much all human beings do them, but they are fantastic, even miraculous accomplishments nonetheless. As a parent you are "in" the trees and it is difficult to step back and see the entire forest. As a grandparent I am able to see the big picture and observe how my words, actions, and intentional modeling directly relate to the development of children.

All of the chapters in this book are part of a plan you can use to determine what kind of household you want and what kind of father you want to be. For lack of a better term, they are tools you can use to develop the foundation to help you become the kind of father you want to be and the kind of father your children deserve. They are a road map that can guide you around some of the issues that can derail you in important areas of fathering and parenting. These are things you might not have previously thought of as important, but utilizing them can kick your fathering skills up a notch or two. For purposes of clarity throughout the book we'll use the term *better dads* for men who are perhaps untrained, average, or even exceptional fathers but who are striving to be even more.

If you want to be a better dad and raise great kids, focus on the practical and easy-to-follow steps and tips outlined in this book. In addition, men can work with other dads in group settings with the accompanying Better Dads Workbook. I highly recommend that approach, as iron truly sharpens iron. And look for the opportunity to work directly with me in our father-to-father mentoring program described at the end of this book.

Good luck—I'm looking forward to seeing the difference you make in your families, communities, and the world!

1

Have Fun!

The Importance of Humor and Play

> Happy families resemble one another, whereas each unhappy family is unhappy in its own tragic way.
>
> —Leo Tolstoy, *Anna Karenina*

Dads are sort of the GPS unit of the family. As Dad goes, so goes the family. So even though fathering may be difficult and even demanding, excellent dads—or at least *better* dads—find ways to make this challenge fun and exciting. They take the attitude that even though it's difficult, it's worth every effort required. Then they find ways to make it fun, and not just a job. You only get one go-round with each kid—and that time goes quicker than you think possible—so you might as well make it as memorable as possible. The satisfaction and joy you'll get in return is well worth every effort you make.

Gauging Your Household Health by the Amount of Laughter

A home with a lot of laughter in it is a healthy home. But happy families do not happen by accident. Here's my question to you: *What is your vision for your family and how are you going to accomplish that vision?*

The first part of developing a vision depends upon determining your goals. Here is a good starting goal you might want to consider. First of all, what are your (and your wife's) career goals? How will you accomplish those goals? They need to be realistic if you want to be a great dad. I can guarantee that you can't be a great dad and work ninety hours a week for twenty years. I don't care how special you are—that's not going to happen.

I've closely studied the lives of many great men throughout history. Some of those men were good fathers, and some were not. But I suspect most of their children would say that they missed their fathers and yearned to have more time with them. The history books don't often come right out and say they were absent from home too much, but if you read between the lines, you can see that they couldn't have accomplished the goals that led to their greatness without expending large amounts of time and passion in pursuit of those goals. It is extremely difficult to spend the time required to achieve great accomplishments and still have time left over to adequately nurture a family. I know a few men who have done it, but not very many.

Next, determine with your wife what you want the tone of your home to be like. Will it be spontaneous and fun or deliberate and serious? What will be the important things that you focus on in your home? Will it be education, character, spirituality, good times, or some combination of all? You'll have to be intentional in nurturing any or all of those things in your home, because likely, they will not just happen.

Why Kids Need Dad's Humor

While the topic of this chapter is the "health" of our family through the amount of laughter, perhaps we could just as easily determine the "wealth" of our family by the amount of laughter and vitality it possesses. The opposite of depression is not happiness—the opposite of depression is vitality. *Vitality* is defined as a healthy life force. A key component of developing vitality is humor. Surveys of children find the number one thing they appreciate most about Dad is his sense of humor. A dad's goofiness helps make life in the family fun and happy. Laughter is one of a dad's greatest tools.

Laughter is underrated. Laughter opens up the way for conversations and it gets people to let down their guard. Your wife was probably initially attracted to you because you made her laugh. Want to get your sullen teens to open up and share something? Get them to laugh and watch how their attitude changes. Even fickle and depressed teenagers want to be around a home that has fun and lots of laughter. Most kids (teens aside) can't wait for Dad to get home because he brings excitement and the outside world home with him. Use that eagerness to share with them funny stories and odd experiences you have throughout the day.

You can gauge the mood or temperature of your household by the amount of laughter that is present. Dads, don't take yourselves so seriously. Yes, life is hard. But it's hard for children too. Your entire family needs to laugh together to bond and grow closer.

Laughter releases chemicals that are mentally and physically healthy. A good hearty belly laugh releases endorphins, the brain's feel-good chemical. Endorphins allow us to ignore pain and relax.[1] Additionally, chemicals such as serotonin and dopamine, which produce the feeling of well-being and contentment, are released in the body by laughter.

As a father, you set the tone of the home for your family. There are times when you will need to be serious and even stern. But I would encourage you to promote laughter in your home as often as possible.

Finding Humor in Life

If you want to have fun with your family, you are going to have to make a conscious decision to do so. Why? Because having fun together takes time. That means you will have to take time away from something else in your life—probably work, but maybe your golf or basketball games. As mentioned earlier, the truth is you probably cannot be *highly* successful both as a father and at work. I know a few men with remarkable talent who work from home and are able to spend enough quality time with their kids. But most guys have to find a balance in their work and home life. Having dinner together every night, going to ball games and recitals, watching a movie and eating popcorn at night together are all things that kids need and cherish on a consistent basis. It's not that you *can't* do both work and home successfully,

Ideas for Creating Fun at Various Ages

- Infants: play peekaboo, make faces or funny noises, "raspberry" their belly, tickle them, put things on your head, or "steal" their nose.
- Toddlers: do most of the stuff you do with babies plus play horsey (either on the floor or with your knee), chase them, play "Where'd so-and-so go?" give them "airplane" rides, or throw them in the air and catch them.
- Grade-school age: tickle (still), wrestle on the floor, perform magic tricks; practical jokes go over well; knock-knock jokes are good.
- Teens: probably don't want to play much with Dad but you can still occasionally engage them in water fights, basketball games like HORSE, or video game competitions. For teen girls try things like taking them to lunch, going on a date, taking them shopping—find things *they* like to do.
- And if you are a grandpa, you can always play the classic "pull my finger" game, which is good for a laugh no matter how old they get (at least it is for boys—it's only fun for girls until they get old enough to tell on you to Mom and Grandma). Or maybe that game is only fun for grandpas.

it's just that most men need to be aware of the sacrifices necessary.

Find fun places to go together—even . . . especially . . . if they are hokey or silly. We go to miniature golf courses, county fairs, renaissance fairs, air shows, arcades, concerts, car shows, gun shows, antique shows, and amusement parks. We also enjoy plenty of physical activities like hiking, camping, rafting, biking, walking, hunting, and fishing.

As dads we make a conscious choice every day to either spend our time and energy nurturing our wives and children or let that energy get directed into work, hobbies, television, or other endeavors. If we use our natural creativity and channel our inner "boy," we can come up with plenty of fun stuff our whole family will enjoy.

Most of all it is attitude. Do you enjoy life? Having a good attitude means finding things to be thankful for. I'm in my midfifties and I'm thankful that I still have some hair on my head—even though a good portion of it has slid from my forehead down my back. Seriously though, I'm very thankful that I'm married to a *good* woman and wife and that my kids have grown into compassionate adults with a strong moral foundation. Recognizing that makes me appreciate my life and have a more enthusiastic outlook and demeanor.

Even if your personality tends to be a little more reserved, you can still find things to joke about or amuse your family with. Always try to find something to laugh about with your kids (but not at their expense). If your personality is such that you are not naturally a joker, find some humorous books or articles to read with your children. Relate experiences where you goofed up as a kid. Tell them stories of things that happened at work or while running errands. Even if you work as an accountant, funny things happen.

Better dads look for ways to make their children laugh. Besides, women seem to get turned on by a man who makes them laugh. Your wife is watching.

What Life Lessons Do Humor and Fun Teach?

When a dad can laugh at himself, then he's worth following. The world is hard, but laughter makes it easier. To laugh in the face of adversity takes courage and even a good bit of bravado. To persevere with a good attitude through

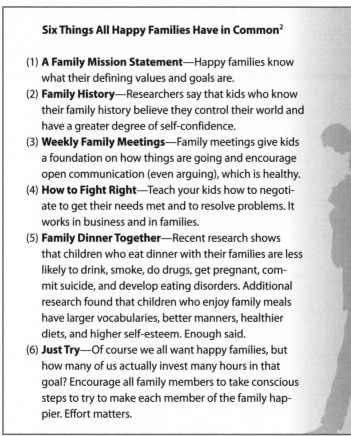

Six Things All Happy Families Have in Common[2]

(1) **A Family Mission Statement**—Happy families know what their defining values and goals are.
(2) **Family History**—Researchers say that kids who know their family history believe they control their world and have a greater degree of self-confidence.
(3) **Weekly Family Meetings**—Family meetings give kids a foundation on how things are going and encourage open communication (even arguing), which is healthy.
(4) **How to Fight Right**—Teach your kids how to negotiate to get their needs met and to resolve problems. It works in business and in families.
(5) **Family Dinner Together**—Recent research shows that children who eat dinner with their families are less likely to drink, smoke, do drugs, get pregnant, commit suicide, and develop eating disorders. Additional research found that children who enjoy family meals have larger vocabularies, better manners, healthier diets, and higher self-esteem. Enough said.
(6) **Just Try**—Of course we all want happy families, but how many of us actually invest many hours in that goal? Encourage all family members to take conscious steps to try to make each member of the family happier. Effort matters.

life's hardships takes resiliency. Having fun, despite life's difficulties, rallies and inspires followers to admire and respect the leader.

Why do you think two of the fourteen character traits in the Boy Scout Law are "friendly" and "cheerful"? Both traits make other people around us feel better about themselves and create a relaxed and welcoming environment. I'd much rather be around happy people than unhappy people, wouldn't you? Plus, your home should be your favorite place to be. A happy home is one that your kids and their friends want to be at as well.

Our home must be over-the-top happy; we're having a hard time getting rid of kids—they keep coming back.

Being able to laugh about life when things are falling apart around us gives your children confidence and hope in our fallen world (and in an imperfect dad). Laughter and happiness help create a positive attitude in children. And a positive attitude is one of the key components to living a good life.

Dad, the way you face life is the way your children will grow up believing they should face life. Life has a way of knocking us down. When that happens, always try to show your children your good face.

Physical Fun

When my kids were little, I remember getting into monster "rassling" matches in the evening with them. I would be in the middle of the living room on my knees and they would come flying as fast as they could before launching themselves headfirst at me. The consequence of a child being captured by the "bear" was a whisker rub on a soft cheek or a strenuous "noogie." They would scream with peals of laughter as the bear chased them on hands and knees while they careened around corners and accidently ran into furniture because they were looking back, not watching where they were going. Mom often had to leave the room, as it got to be too much for her. We all suffered minor bumps and bruises, but we would all admit it was worth it.

Dads who engage in roughhousing with their kids teach them a number of very important skills in life. Kids who wrestle around on the floor with Dad develop portions of their brain, muscles, and reflexes; they also gain psychological benefits. Roughhousing actually rewires a child's brain in a variety of ways. It develops neural pathways within the brain that help a child be flexible in their thinking and adapt to unexpected situations—which happen frequently in life. Next, wrestling releases chemicals within the brain that help develop memory, logic, and higher learning functions. Roughhousing also increases a child's social intelligence. It helps them differentiate between play and real aggression, a distinction with which many children struggle. It teaches kids to deal with pain and discomfort. The inadvertent bumps and scrapes they get while wrestling with Dad help them deal with those types of stresses when they are in school. It also teaches the development of morals, cooperation, and boundaries in children. It teaches kids rules—if you kick Dad "there," serious repercussions occur.

Dads also contribute significantly to the physical condition of their children. A dad who is in good shape tends to have children who are physically fit as well. A father's level of activity directly contributes to his child's level of activity. So wrestling with your children helps them be in good physical condition. Roughhousing is a great bonding mechanism as well. Hopefully it includes a great deal of physical affection, which is healthy to a child's self-esteem and well-being. It also builds trust. When you throw your child up in the air (provided you catch him), it teaches your child that they can trust you. Last, it teaches them the rewards that come from taking risks—which is a big part of being successful in life.

Kids not only need and love wrestling and horseplaying with Dad, but it gives them confidence and security. Getting close to and touching Dad gives them access to your masculine "essence" that children need. A man's physicality provides calmness and security to children. At our single moms' family camps, many of the young boys show up the first day angry and acting out. By the next evening around the campfire many will crawl up onto the laps of the male volunteers (some of the boys sucking their thumbs in contentment) and you can literally watch them nuzzle into the chests of the men, absorbing the masculine essence that they have been craving. They are calm, contented, and happy.

All children need the touch of a father or father figure. It's just sometimes easier to see it by how it affects children when it is absent from their lives.

Physical Affection

Roughhousing with your kids is a great opportunity for laughter, but it also provides you a chance to show physical affection. All children crave healthy masculine affection. They need it so much that their lives are blessed if they have it. But it's such a strong need that if they don't have healthy masculine affection in their lives they will accept unhealthy masculine affection in its place. So young girls who do not get healthy affection from their fathers will confuse sex for love in the backseats of cars, and young men with no father to guide them will join gangs of other fatherless boys searching for the affirmation, validation, and affection they need from older males.

Learning to show affection was initially difficult for me. I grew up in a home where neither my mother nor father gave out much physical affection. But it was something I intuitively knew I missed. So when my children were born, I was determined to give them the physical affection I had desired. This was uncomfortable at first, as I had never had those behaviors modeled (yeah, I know—kissing and hugging ain't rocket science). But I forced myself to try as often as possible to give my kids a lot of hugs and kisses. I'm really glad I did. It has opened doors in the relationships with my children now as adults that probably would have been closed had I not. Additionally, those actions on my part spoke "words" of love to my children that I might not have been capable of articulating.

Guys, if you don't give your son the physical affection he needs, it will be difficult to develop a deeper relationship with him. With boys this might mean hugs and kisses, but often a simple arm around the shoulders, a pat on the back, or a head "noogie" works just as well.

If your daughter doesn't get healthy physical affection from her father while growing up, she *will* eventually seek that masculine affection she craves from other sources—usually ones you don't want giving her physical affection. We have to walk a bit of a tightrope in this area, as when our daughters reach puberty, it becomes more difficult to understand how to meet their needs for healthy affection. Typically this is the time when dads and daughters' relationships often drift apart or become uncomfortable (if not downright adversarial). Dad tends to get a little freaked out by his baby girl's impending sexuality, and with hormones and other chemicals flowing through her newly maturing body, your daughter may not want Dad touching her either. Even just giving her a hug becomes awkward. It's important to respect her wishes in this area but also that she know you are available for a hug whenever she needs or wants one. Oftentimes words of affirmation, life wisdom, and encouragement to a daughter during this time period serve as well as physical affection. Regardless, men, don't allow your awkwardness with her approaching womanhood to deter you from keeping a close relationship. This is the time she needs you most! She will need you now more than ever before as she navigates through the treacherous waters of adolescence. This is a time (especially for girls) when her choices can become a blessing to her or have painful lifelong consequences. Don't be absent when she needs you to fight for her most.

Better dads give their kids plenty of hugs and kisses—even if they are uncomfortable giving physical affection.

Playing

This past Christmas my son gave me the best present any middle-aged man could ever want. He gave me a Nerf N-Strike Vulcan EBF-25 Dart Cannon. It looks and operates like an orange and yellow 50-caliber machine gun. It even has an ammo box that you load the belt into and it feeds out the other side as the darts are fired by an internal piston-powered launching system. The Vulcan fires up to three Nerf sonic micro darts per second (although not confirmed by my testing) and has a 25-round ammo belt. In fully auto mode it can fire all twenty-five rounds in under ten seconds. Very, very cool indeed! My son was wise enough to get me a second ammo belt to go along with it.

After running out to get the required six C cell batteries, I played "war" with my son until he got tired and went home. I spent the rest of the day "hunting" the cats. They were fast but not fast enough to outrun a determined middle-aged man with a machine gun. The dog is no fun, as he just stands there and lets me shoot him. I am working on building a pill box with pillows to create a machine gun nest using the tripod stand that came with it. I started saving to buy the Tactical Rail accessories that go with it, including a laser sight and flashlight so I can hunt our cats throughout the house in the dark.

I was also coveting the other N-Strike arsenal weapons, including the giant pistol Maverick with 6-dart rotating barrel that looks like it came from a *Terminator* movie and the N-Strike Recon CS-6 Blaster, which as near as I can tell is a Nerf assault shotgun. Lo and behold, the next morning I found out the little guys next door had gotten those very items for Christmas! Oh, what great battles we had in the cul-de-sac that day. If we would have had toys like this when I was a kid, I would have never come home.

The best thing about dads is that we are men, and men are really just big boys—we never get tired of playing. Find some cool stuff to play with your kids. They have so many cool toys that we never even dreamed of when I was growing up. Remote control helicopters! You heard me—remote control helicopters! Need I say anything more? The boys next door have a battery-powered Jeep they ride around the neighborhood in—and it goes pretty fast. On his birthday last month one of the boys got a motorized skateboard. If that's not about the coolest thing I've ever seen, I don't know what is. Unfortunately, it isn't powerful enough to motor my fat behind around the cul-de-sac (the mom was frowning at me out the window for almost breaking her kid's toy).

I don't know what kind of cool toys are out there now for girls because I only peruse the boys' section of the toy aisles in the store. But they must have some things now that would even impress a dad.

Spend some time playing with your kids. Not only will you bond with them, it will lower your stress level and blood pressure.

2

Go Outside Your Comfort Zone

But It's Uncomfortable Out Here!

All it takes for a contagious manly culture to form is for one genuine man to live out genuine manhood.

—Stephen Mansfield

It's been said that manly men do manly things. But to be an effective father, sometimes we have to engage in activities that make us uncomfortable (and may even feel somewhat unmanly) in order to get to know our children better. There's probably not a father of little girls who at one time or another has not either played Barbie, had curlers put in his hair, or had his fingernails painted by his little "princesses." I'll never forget the time I walked in on my very tall and reserved father sitting at a tiny table in my daughter's room playing "tea party" with a three-sizes-too-small ladies' straw hat perched on top of his head. It was so out of character for him that we were both stunned for a moment. I ran to grab a camera, and I cherish that picture of him sitting at the table with a rather hangdog look on his face, being directed by my confidently bossy little daughter.

By being willing to engage our kids on their level and in the things that they enjoy doing, this allows us to bond with them deeper. Time spent together on their level, in their environment, allows us to get to know them as a person—the person they *are*, not the one we *think* they are (or wish they were).

Men who as boys felt neglected by their dads are often distant from their own children. Since it hurts to be neglected, we then tend to question our value to others. So to avoid feeling the sting of further rejection, we refuse to give that part of ourselves we fear might once again be received with indifference.[1] If you were in that situation, guys, don't pass that wound on to your children. They shouldn't have to pay for someone else's mistakes. Be intentional about breaking that generational cycle. As I mentioned before, I recognized early that I missed out by not having a close, loving relationship with my parents. I made a pact with myself to do whatever I could, no matter how uncomfortable it was, to have a close relationship with my children. That meant I forced myself initially to give them a lot of physical affection (hugs and kisses), which I wasn't particularly comfortable with because it had never been modeled for me as a child. It also meant that I went places I didn't want to go and even did things I probably considered undignified, all in an effort to spend time in their environments. This allowed me to get to know them on a deeper, rather than superficial, level and helped me to understand what motivated them and how best to reach and teach each of them. Fatherhood requires sacrifice and oftentimes courage. It's a noble challenge, although maybe it's not so much a sacrifice as it is just having our priorities straight.

When men become fathers, they chose to sacrifice parts of their lives for the benefit of their family. They put aside their personal goals, dreams, and ambitions in order to devote those energies to lifting up the lives of their wives and children. When grandparents choose to raise their grandchildren, they put aside those long-delayed goals and dreams to focus on the children as well. They also forfeit their roles as grandparents in order to fulfill the role of a parent. We make those sacrifices without pride because that's what good men do—it's what fathers, grandfathers, uncles, and mentors do.

Regardless, I can't tell you how many roller-coaster rides I've been on, birthday parties with clowns I've attended, or lousy pizzas I've eaten that were served by a mouse, but it's been a lot. And speaking of uncomfortable situations, if I had a nickel for every poopie diaper I've changed, I'd be living in a villa on the beach in the Bahamas.

Explore Unfamiliar Things with Your Child (Go Places and Do Things You Wouldn't Normally Do)

Go places with your children that you are uncomfortable with or unused to going to. This puts you on the same footing as your kids and allows you to explore things together as equals. It's a great way to bond with each other. I'll have to admit, I'm not known as a real big step-out-of-your-comfort-zone kind of guy. Nevertheless I tried my best to do things I wasn't thrilled about doing. I figured if I can manage the nerve to get onstage in front of thousands of people, the least I can do is step outside my comfort zone with my kids occasionally. You do brave things all the time at work or with hobbies—don't be afraid to have the courage to go places where children rule.

Get used to taking your teenage daughter shopping for clothes (at the mall, no less). My daughter loved the fact that I paid for her clothes, but she so wasn't thrilled about the fact that I went along to approve what clothing she could buy. That is, until her other friends who did not have dads living at home told her, "I'd give anything just to have my dad around." I drew the line at shopping for brassieres and other unmentionables (her mother got that job), but it is important that dads be involved in how a girl presents herself to the world. Yeah, I know, some of you young guys are going to be calling me old-fashioned or patriarchal (or at least your liberated wives will be), but I've seen the results in the lives of too many young women whose fathers did not care enough to be involved in their lives beyond a cursory level. When your daughter gets old enough to start emulating hypersexual pop stars and you've lost a little more hair, you'll know exactly what I'm talking about.

My wife and daughter just told me they want to go skydiving. I did this when I was a young man, so I don't have any great urge to do it again. But I guess I better suck it up and put my jump boots back on because it looks like I'm leaping out of a plane again.

If you travel for a living, make sure you let your kids know where you are going so they can track where you are in the world. I have a friend who every so often will take one of his children on a business trip with him. His children love it! They get quality one-on-one time with him, plus they get to go on an adventure with Dad! These kinds of trips allow our children to see what our world looks like.

I once spoke at a women's conference where I was the only man in attendance. My wife wasn't free to go with me, and since it wasn't a good idea for me to be hanging around a couple thousand women all by myself, I asked my daughter to accompany me. Even as a young adult, you'd have thought she hit the lottery jackpot. We flew to Southern California, stayed in a luxury hotel, and were escorted around by a bevy of people wanting to serve us. My daughter was very professional, did a great job, and was even pretty protective of her dad. She got a chance to see what my world looked like and how I did my job. Plus she got to bond with me on an adventure. For the longest time she kept a "selfie" of us at the airport on her cell phone home screen.

Step into Your Kids' Comfort Zones Occasionally (Their School, Hangouts, Friends, etc.)

Hey, Dad! When was the last time you visited your kids' school when it wasn't parent-teacher conferences, a ball game, or a recital? Go spend a day hanging out in the school and your children's classrooms (maybe even just show up unannounced for lunch occasionally). They always need volunteers, and adult males are seldom seen in public schools. You not only give a gift of your presence to your own children, but to all the other boys and girls who never see a positive male role model. Anecdotal evidence shows that men in schools provide a very calming influence in the classroom. You might be surprised how well you are received. Boys especially thrive under male tutelage. Besides, schools need to hear the voices of fathers. Since mothers are more involved with school, all the schools ever hear is a mother's perspective. Not only is it important to have a male perspective presented, but because school administrators and teachers seldom hear from men, your word carries a lot of weight.

Invite your children's friends to come along with your family on different events. Yes, it can be a pain, but having their friends along lets you get a glimpse into your child's world. Be respectful to their friends and treat them as part of the family. Our goal was to make our kids and their friends want to come over to our house or along with us so that we had at least some control over the environment and what they were being exposed to. The other side to that is, you never know who you are influencing or how your influence affects them. Boys and girls without dads in the home (or with poor role models) desperately need positive male role models to judge men and boys against and offset any negative impressions.

Besides, your children will often behave better with a friend along because they know you'll tell on them about something they'd rather the entire school didn't know about.

Enter Their World

My kids always wanted to go places that were guaranteed to set my teeth on edge—usually loud, busy, crowded, noisy pizza parlors with plenty of flashing lights and loud bells and whistles that smelled like little kids' sweat and the vomit from too much sugar. We also attended a lot of concerts where adults onstage sang whacky songs that stuck in your head for days afterward. As they got older, their video arcades smelled of puberty and teenage angst. Ever smelled the inside of a roller skating rink? Take the smell of a video arcade and add the smell of stinky socks and you'll know what I'm talking about.

If you aren't willing to go places they want to go and interact with them in their world, you'll never have critical and important conversations with them. They usually won't talk to you about those kinds of things on your level. Especially as they get older, you have to make time for them and intentionally create situations that put you face-to-face with them in their environment. And the best conversations always happen when you are *doing* something together—not when you sit them down for a "talk." This is good news for us dads, because as males we can talk better while doing something than we can sitting down across the table from someone. We also bond easier by doing things together with another person.

Of course, if we want to speak into our kids' lives, we have to earn the right to be heard. We earn that right by being respected by our children. Unfortunately, respect doesn't grow on trees. We have to work at developing respect just like we do in any other aspect of our lives or relationships. That means we have to treat *them* with respect. We have to be firm but fair in our decision making. We have to be intentional in monitoring and filtering the volume, tone, and kinds of words that come out of our mouths. If we are abusive, we run the risk of losing their respect. And respect lost is more difficult to get back than it is to earn in the first place.[2] Can I just say that the biggest reason I see fathers losing their children's respect is by not enforcing consistent boundaries in their children's lives. Giving in and allowing them to get what they want whenever they put up a fuss is a surefire way to lose their respect.

If you've lost the respect of your children (no matter their age), you might start by offering a sincere, heartfelt apology, followed by asking for their forgiveness. Then be intentional about earning their respect, just like you would your wife, your friends, or a boss or co-worker.

Having their respect makes having those difficult conversations much easier. Like having the sex talks (yes, plural because one is never enough). These are uncomfortable at best with your son, much less your daughter. But those are exactly the kinds of conversations kids need to have with their fathers. Boys need to get straight talk on how a man deals with his sexuality. Girls need to hear from a man how males think about sex and what healthy male sexuality looks like. If you don't "set the table" early in their life, these kinds of conversations are much more difficult.

Travel—Making Memories through Adventures

It struck me the other day that we seldom know when we are making history. Yes, Neil Armstrong knew when he was the first man to walk on the moon that he was making history. But most of the time I think we just do things and somehow end up getting swept up into the history books. Did Rosa Parks set out to make a world-changing statement by refusing to sit in the back of the bus? Probably not—she was just tired and fed up and wanted to sit down. Or do you think when Davy Crockett moseyed down to a little former Spanish mission, he had any idea he would be martyred in maybe

Favorite Adventures with Dad (from readers)

- Riding in a helicopter on the World's Most Famous Beach (Daytona Beach).
- Getting up at 4:00 a.m. to go fishing (we took ham & onion sandwiches).
- Daddy/daughter dances—we attended many over the years. We dressed up and went on a "date."
- My dad sold sporting goods products. He used to take me to all those old-fashioned boxing gyms. I still remember the unique odor they all had—a combination of sweat, blood, spit, fear, and liniment.
- Sitting at the table listening to him conduct family Bible study each week (I hated it then, but the foundation is invaluable now as I am rearing my own children).

the most famous battle in Texas history and that his death would cement his legend in frontier folklore? I suspect he didn't believe he would die at the Alamo; he just went down to do what he thought was right at the time.

I think most people who do significant things in life probably do not do them under the premise of creating history. Most are ordinary people who just do something (usually the right thing for the right reason) and find themselves at the convergence of a number of crossroads that come together to make a significant event. The key word is *do*—they *do* something. You can't accomplish anything if you never do anything. You can't make a history for your family by being at work or watching TV all the time.

One of the regrets I have is that we did not take enough family vacations. Yes, we took the obligatory trips to the beach or mountains several times a year, but we only took a couple of "two-week, travel to a different country" kind of adventures. As a small business owner, to me it always seemed that when I had the time to do those kinds of trips, I didn't have the money, and when I had the money, I didn't have the time.

But those trips (uncomfortable for me—either physically or economically) tended to be the ones we all remembered the most. The weeklong wilderness camping trips I took with my kids, the hunting trips with my son, the family vacation to Mexico, and the 2,500-mile road trip across Western America were all ones we still talk about today.

Some of the adventures with our children included the following:

1. My son and I had great times deer hunting from the time he was eleven through eighteen years old. We hunted both by ourselves and with groups of other fathers and sons. These were unique and often powerful times of males bonding in nature. I would have been willing to take my daughter, but she did not have much interest in shooting a "poor little deer."
2. Over the years we have had a great time as a family going shooting together. Sometimes we go as a family, other times I just take either one or both children with me. Sometimes my wife and I will even sneak off on a date and shoot a few rounds. We shoot pistols, rifles, and shotguns. This has been a fun and educational experience for everyone.
3. Over the years the kids were growing up, I would take one or the other every summer on a wilderness camping trip. This is where we would pick a remote wilderness

location and hike in with backpacks. Since we could not carry much food, we lived on the fish we caught and any freeze-dried food we packed in. We had some hugely memorable trips doing this. One of the best was when I and several other fathers all brought our teen girls up in the Three Sisters Wilderness area. Having four fifteen-year-old girls in the wilderness with no toilet was quite an adventure. But the girls were great sports and had as good a time as the dads. Every time I run across one of these adult women now, they always mention that trip and how much fun it was.

4. Our family went on numerous camping trips, weekend trips to the beach, resort trips, whitewater rafting trips, and skiing or sledding adventures. We also occasionally went snowboarding, snowshoeing, or cross-country skiing.

Frankly, if I'm being honest I have to admit that my wife was the motivating force behind many of these adventures. I was often focused on working or getting ahead in life and needed her to remind me to take time to spend with the kids and family.

If I had it to do over again, I like to think I'd go on more epic family vacations to create memories that would warm me in my old age. I think I would have been a better dad if I had.

Find a Common Cause or Enemy

One thing that draws people close together is having a common cause. I'm not advocating that you and your children find someone to hate. But I am suggesting you find some things you can join together to battle against or work on together. For my family, it was working together in my ministry. The enemy we fought against was fatherlessness and the devastation it causes in the lives of women and children. Your enemy might be any number of social injustices that you all agree are worthy causes to fight against. Our family participated in several prayer vigils outside abortion clinics and served at a number of soup kitchens. Other causes might involve human trafficking, poverty, racism, genocide, domestic violence, or just about anything you and your family have a passion for.

You might also find some personal causes to work on together as a family. Maybe you would like your family to eat better and exercise more with the goal of losing weight and being healthier. The enemy in this case is obesity, laziness, and discouragement. Together you work to slay the enemy. You could also have a goal of growing spiritually as a family. We all know who the enemy of that goal would be.

Gather ideas from each family member on how to grow in any of these areas and what a plan of action might look like. Having the whole family work together on a common goal creates buy-in and gives them ownership. Some of these things might be a bit uncomfortable initially, but I promise you'll be glad you did once you get started. Nothing draws a family closer than working together serving others and making a difference in the world. You'll be a better dad because of it.

3

Surround Yourself with Healthy Friends and Couples

It Matters!

> The greatest gift you can give to somebody is your own personal development. I used to say, "If you will take care of me, I will take care of you." Now I say, "I will take care of me for you, if you will take care of you for me."
>
> —Jim Rohn

The family is under assault like never before. In his iconic 1951 book on the strategies used to create mass movements (communism, socialism, progressivism, radical religion, etc.), *The True Believer*, Eric Hoffer says this:

> Almost all of our contemporary movements showed in their early stages a hostile attitude toward the family, and did all

> they could to discredit and disrupt it. They did it by undermining the authority of the parents; by facilitating divorce; by taking over responsibility for feeding, educating and entertaining the children; and by encouraging illegitimacy.[1]

Our culture today seems to be attempting to do those very things to the family. We desperately need friends and family who have the same values as we do to come alongside us and help support us and our children as we go through the challenges of life. I believe that to be true today, regardless of your value system.

Today, families are isolated—we live without any social networks, and I'm not talking about internet social networks. How many of us live near our families or even know our neighbors? The model for parenting today is performed by two inexperienced biological parents who work full-time and parent part-time. Throughout history, extended families lived together as a unit, raising children together. We are the first parents in all of history to raise and educate an entire generation of young people without the active involvement of networks of grandparents, aunts, uncles, cousins, nephews, neighbors, in-laws, and friends. Without this adult interaction, our kids have turned to their peers for behavioral points of reference.[2] Unfortunately, children can't teach other children to become mature adults—only mature adults can do that.

I also think most men today are lonely. Author Joe Kita says, "The ironic thing about this is I'm not alone in my loneliness. I see lots of other men just like me whose entire lives are career and family. Hanging around with the guys is a childish, troublesome thing that interferes with being a good husband, father, and role model."[3] But it shouldn't be that way. Men need friends. We need other men we can be ourselves around—to let down that guard that we always have surrounding us, to escape the pressure of always being "on."

As a married couple, surround yourself with the "right" kind of people—other married couples, family members, and friends who encourage each other, hold one another accountable, and care about you and your family. The people in your inner circle (friends or family) will influence your children. Make sure it is the influence you want it to be—choose your friends wisely. If you don't have a circle of like-minded people, it is you against the world for the hearts and minds of your children. Better dads know those are bad odds.

Why Do Men Struggle Making Friendships?

Friendship requires a certain degree of vulnerability. To most men, vulnerability is not masculine, and so we avoid it. It's hard enough to be vulnerable with your wife, let alone with another man. But without vulnerability you never really grow close. You're associates with other men—maybe even close ones. But to be a real friend you have to be honest with where you are, with what you're feeling (another weak point to the masculine ego), and be willing to accept the possibility that the other person might think you're too touchy-feely. Frankly, we are not always sure if we let our guard down with another man that he will reciprocate, or he may even use it against us at some point (men being as competitive with one another as they are). Men hesitate to share their struggles with one another because they think sharing a problem is whining about it, and not being able to fix your own problems is somehow unmanly. One thing we tend to forget is that most of us struggle with the exact same problems. Our difficulties are never as unique as we think they are—it's part of the human condition.

Not only that, but our culture seems suspicious of male friendship. Male friendships have an aura of homosexual overtones as seen by society at large and other males in particular. Men might be concerned that by drawing too close to another male they will be perceived as gay or too feminine. A David-Jonathan friendship between two men would probably be met with scorn and mockery by most of our culture today. In addition, there is a school of thought in America that if groups of men band together, it is somehow dangerous. One only need look at the flack that groups like Promise Keepers and any other men-only organizations get from the secular media and feminist women's groups.

Finding new friends gets harder as you get older, but it is not impossible. Common values seem to be the number one attribute that unites men, more even than common interests. But if time is required to establish deep friendships, the older you get, the less of it you have, so I suspect the number of really close friends winnows itself down naturally.

Also our roles in friendships can change over the years. And friendship can be confusing to most men. One man told me,

> I do have a couple of very close friends—men who can speak the truth to me even if I'm screwing up—sort of a Nathan to David. It takes time to develop that. I've been having breakfast with one guy for forty years every Friday morning when we're both in town. I used to think I was the mentee and he was the mentor, but after his wife died last year and he asked me to do the memorial service, I've found that in our old age he is looking to me as much as I have looked to him for the past four decades. I think we're friends.

10 Reasons Why Men Have So Much Difficulty Making Friends[4]
(reasons given by men for why they don't have more friends)

(1) *We're too busy*—Friendships take time. Who has time today to nurture a long-term relationship?
(2) *We're too selfish*—"What's in it for me?" is often the primary criteria on whether men should build a relationship with someone.
(3) *We're too functional*—Male friendships typically grow out of organizations—work, sports, clubs. When our participation ends, so do the friendships.
(4) *We're too proud*—Men think, "I can manage life on my own. I don't need friends."
(5) *We're too fearful*—We don't want anyone to think we are gay.
(6) *We're too safe*—We are not prepared to risk rejection. Better to stay safely at arm's length than try to get closer and risk being rejected.
(7) *We're too superficial*—Friendships thrive where there is real authenticity, where both parties let down their guard and show real emotions and feelings.
(8) *We're too brainwashed*—TV and Hollywood portray a real man as strong and stoic. He is a loner who safely fits in society's "Man Box."
(9) *We're too competitive*—Who wants to be friends with someone who is always best at something, wants everyone to know, and never encourages or praises anyone else?
(10) *We're too un-Christlike*—Jesus's friendships (12 strong ones in just a few years) were motivated by a desire to serve and do friends eternal and spiritual good.

Interesting, isn't it, that this man didn't really know if they were friends even after forty years of sharing the most intimate details of their lives together. It speaks to the struggles men have in generating friendships in their lives.

Male friendships are cemented over time; they take time to set and harden. Much like concrete, a friendship cures over time, depending on a variety of factors like temperament and personality, time together, frequency of physical activities, willingness to share openly, trust, and exposure to significant challenges in each other's lives. Often this process takes place through shared experiences. It might include going fishing, climbing a mountain, or working on a service project together. Friendship, much like discipleship, takes time, as men are slow to take down their guard. Unlike women who can make a great friend in a day, men seem to have to figure each other out before they can relax and be themselves. For many men fear is always just below the surface—image is a big factor. *What will others think of me? Will they make fun of me? Can I trust them?* These are thoughts that consciously or even unconsciously go through a man's mind when he sizes up potential friends.

Certainly it is more difficult for men to make friends than for women. A man's friends tend to be friends from childhood, high school, or college. As he gets older, it seems to be more difficult to spend the time and effort seeking and cultivating friendships. Men, though, do deeply desire masculine friendships.

Here is what that struggle looks like to one man and how he tries to address it:

> This is something I have always struggled with. Again, moving around a lot growing up didn't help me in this category and I have found that I get envious when I see other men who have great friends from childhood. I struggled to put together a team of guys who I thought would be groomsmen for my wedding. That was embarrassing.

> Over the past few years I have made a point to get to know other guys and reach out to spend time with guys for small events such as sporting events, concerts, grilling out, etc. I have found that most guys want to do this, but they don't know how to reach out.

Most men have lots of acquaintances, but only a few close friends in their inner circle. To males, friendship often consists of like-mindedness, meaning they have something in common they like to do together. Men who are friends "do life" together. Since males tend to bond through physical experiences rather than verbal communication, friendship typically involves doing things together. When guys can work on a common goal or a shared experience together, it greatly speeds up the bonding process.

Here's one man's advice on making friends:

> I don't make friends easily. My boy inherited that unfortunate trait from me. But my six-year-old daughter educated me on how to make friends. She said to walk up to someone that looks lonely, tell them your name, and then ask them if they want to be your friend. Not sure that works for a fifty-year-old man, but I took that advice to heart. Out of the mouth of babes comes truth and wisdom.

Another man responded this way when asked how he makes friends:

> I find new friends in the activities my wife and I share together, i.e., small groups, or neighborhood, school, new job. I am not on the hunt for new friends nor have I ever been because I will want to invest in the relationship. If my life is loaded with stuff, this new friend will be found in these activities. Getting to my inner circle requires the building up

> of trust and time. One does not just become friends and get in my inner circle. My inner circle of guys know all my stuff (good and bad) and are a help when the sledding gets tough.

Being isolated is dangerous to men and to our families. Better dads don't allow that to happen.

Why Dads (and Men) Need Quality Friends

Most men have plenty of male acquaintances, but very few have close friendships with other men. Does this mean that most men are lonely? I think so. Friendships are healthy for us even though we tend to buy into the myth that we don't need anyone else in our lives or that our wives are our best friends. Human beings tend to be tribal creatures—we function better when we collaborate, teach, affirm, and encourage one another. People who are isolated become insecure and vulnerable to a variety of problems.

Loneliness in males accelerates age-related declines in cognition and motor function. Lonely people (most often men) have chronically elevated levels of the stress and fear hormones cortisol and epinephrine, associated with systematic inflammation, which elevates the risk for viral infection and cardiovascular disease. One good friend can make a ten-year difference in overall life expectancy. A huge meta-study at Brigham Young University found that loneliness is just as harmful to health as not exercising, smoking, or alcoholism and twice as bad as obesity. A 2010 study in the *Journal of Clinical Oncology* studied cancer patients in China. Friendship turned out to be the number one predictor of survival.[5]

I'm convinced that dads with children in the home need friendships with other fathers maybe more during this time of their life than any other. I don't think I've ever met a really good dad who lived in a vacuum. Here's why fathers need to surround themselves with friends and other men they respect. Men need other men to push them. Without that we slump into old habits like lethargy and sloth. We need male friends who inspire us to try new and bold things. Who hold us accountable when we are wrong or want to take shortcuts or even quit. I need young men who still have passion and idealism to combat my older-male jaded cynicism. I also need older friends to give me wisdom and encouragement. And we all need coaching and training as we go throughout life.

I was recently complaining to an older friend of mine about all the struggles life was throwing at me (and they were truly significant). He listened for a while, nodded in understanding, then said something that completely changed my attitude. He said, "You know, Rick, that God will never give you struggles that you cannot handle. Your problem is you are a very tough guy. So God is loading up on you because he knows you can take it."

Wow—from that perspective my problems became much more noble and warrior-like. It became a battle instead of a burden. Upon hearing that story, another friend told me he didn't think that was true—God did in fact often give us more than we were capable of handling. He did it so we would be forced to rely on him. Both perspectives seem true (and very wise) to me.

Another good friend told me something that changed my entire perspective. Since he is a mature man with a young family, I was bemoaning to him the challenges of being a grandfather and having to raise a toddler grandchild. He casually told me something that left me dumbstruck. He said, "Rick, I think that for people like you and me who have a ministry that God is not done using yet, he has a way of keeping us relevant. If you were an empty nester, you couldn't relate to parents with young children." Ouch! What do you say to that except, "You're right."

The point is, though, that without those kinds of men in my life to inspire me, motivate me, and feed me wisdom, I would be likely to quit, self-destruct, or make choices I would later regret.

Why Make the Effort to Find Healthy Couples?

Part of the challenge is to surround ourselves with healthy people—both individual friends and couples. It does us no good to hang around with people who are either negative—bringing us down and making us depressed—or those who give us bad advice. Unfortunately, most people seek out others at their level of emotional and psychological healthiness, thus not associating with people who could offer valuable advice. Have you ever noticed that people (usually family members) who need advice (probably good advice that you could give them) never ask you for advice, but only take the advice of their "loser" friends? I think it's human nature to only ask for advice that we *want* to hear, not the advice we *need* to hear.

We need to shake off that compulsion and find other men who have genuinely good advice and experiences from which we can benefit. That means we have to be humble enough to accept advice we might not want to hear and be corrected when we think we are right. We can't do that if we don't genuinely respect those men. And it's always easier to respect men who are where we want to be, not where we are in life. That prospect can be frightening to most men. Better dads have the courage to face their faults and allow good men to speak into their lives.

Most of us think that networks and support groups are for people with problems or those who are needy. The truth is just the opposite. People with healthy networks and support groups tend to have fewer problems, and those who are isolated tend to develop more serious problems.

Much like close friends, most couples I talk to generally only have one or two close "couple-friends" that they spend time with. Typically those relationships are cultivated by doing things together (going to movies, dinner, vacations, etc.).

Men tend to want to "do" things with their friends—they enjoy the companionship. When I completed the Warrior Dash (a five-kilometer race in land, mud, and water with twelve different obstacles throughout) this past year, my wife asked if I would do it again. I said, "Yes, but only if I can get someone to do it with me." The effort would be a so much more fulfilling and rewarding experience if shared with another guy.

Some of the best times my wife and I have had are with other couples during yearlong home Bible study groups. Many couples develop deeper relationships through these small groups, which encourage sharing deeper issues and problems than we might normally share with a stranger. One woman shared this advice on couple-friends:

> Yes, we have a few close couples in our lives. A few of them we met during our small group Bible study and one we met as friends fourteen years ago during a career function. The

> wife became my best friend fourteen years ago and was inherited in our couples' circle when I remarried a little over a year ago. We cultivate our friendships by being honest with one another, respecting boundaries (although we are good friends, none of us go alone anywhere with the other's mate), we engage in philanthropic and fun stuff together approximately every six weeks or so. We consider that moment a couples' date night. We also don't share any information that should be for our mate's ears only with one another. This maintains a strong level of trust and respect between us as couples and friends!

Those seem like some good rules to abide by if you want lasting friendships with other couples.

What Does **Healthy** *Mean?*

Healthy means we sometimes do things for our spouse and children that we don't want to do. Throughout the course of your marriage, this might change as your roles within the family do. When we first had custody of our baby granddaughter, my wife spent a vast amount of her time taking care of her. That meant someone had to take over housework, the dishes, and laundry. I certainly didn't want to, but since she had greater priorities, I had to step up to the plate. Our roles changed, but as a team we each did what needed to be done (hopefully just for a short season).

Healthy, quality friends are those who can serve as role models or even mentors to us. We respect them and they respect us. They speak truth into our lives even when saying things we do not want to hear. They stand by you even when you are struggling or make mistakes. Those kinds of friends tend to be hard to find today.

How many men like that do you have in your life? If you answered few or none, you need to take an active approach to finding some. The next section discusses how to start. You need men in your life—men whom you can trust to have your best interests and those of your wife and children in mind.

How Do You Find Healthy Friends?

I told my teenage daughter, if you want to meet quality guys you've got to go where they hang out. The same goes for men if we want to find a friend. You don't find a good guy hanging out in a bar or swingers club. But you might find one coaching your kid's Little League team, or leading a Boy Scout troop, or attending a men's group at church, or doing any number of things that make the world a better place. The kind of guys I want to hang around with are doing things to help others—they are using their masculine power to change lives and make the world better. I have one friend who has started an organization that brings volunteer doctors and dentists together to provide free services to the economically disadvantaged community. They put together free events that draw thousands of people from the community and provide them with valuable medical services they couldn't otherwise afford. Another friend helped develop a microbusiness program making and selling soap to help women and children get out of sex trafficking in Lebanon. Still another works with street kids, bringing them hope and encouragement. Several other good friends across the country are engaged in the life-and-death battle of rescuing and supporting sex trafficking victims.

Those are the kind of people I admire. Those involved in helping others always seem to be mentally and emotionally healthier than those who focus on themselves. Since these people clearly care about others, they have no problem caring about me and my family.

Male friendship is a tenuous thing. Unless you grew up with a guy (or group of guys) and shared boyhood adventures and traumas, it's difficult to make good friendships that last. Even men who went through college together as roommates tend to drift apart as the chapters of their lives unfold. I've had several good friendships fade away after I changed my career from business owner to a writer and speaker. It saddens me that some people choose to be threatened by that change instead of celebrating it. Perhaps because it makes them feel guilty or ashamed for not growing themselves. But the truth is some people are in our lives for a season and some for longer periods. Those in our lives for a short time are usually there to teach us something or help us through a situation. They are no less valuable friends than those who are in our lives for a lifetime.

Frankly, women also have a way of interfering with male friendships. Wives and girlfriends seldom like their man's attention and affection being directed away from them, and some feel a man's male friends are a threat. Wives often want their husbands to be *their* best friends, not someone else's. They believe this is what makes the marriage relationship secure. But a team of researchers from around the world found that by the time married women reach forty-five years of age or so, they tend to demote their husbands from first to second place among their most important relationships—typically in favor of an adult daughter or other female.[6] This leaves men who have let youthful friendships pass away stuck without a best friend or often even *any* friends.

Home groups, community activities, hobbies, sports, or even our children's school activities are good places to meet guys to befriend. Any situation or activity that provides a common interest is a good situation to reach out to guys. Understand that sometimes you will be met with rejection. In our isolated culture many men do not know how to make or receive friends. My wife and I made a conscious decision years ago that we would reach out to a wide variety of people as often as possible to try to make friends. We knew we would get rejected a lot (and we have been), but we thought the effort would be worth it. Know that when people choose not to reciprocate your outreach, it is not necessarily a reflection upon you. There are a variety of reasons why people may not accept your offer of friendship, likely having nothing to do with you. Perhaps it's a bad time in their life. Maybe they are too busy, or consumed by their own problems. My point is that it's important not to take things personally. Timing is everything. People who weren't interested in connecting (or at least gave us that impression) when we had previously reached out became good friends later when circumstances in their lives changed.

Having healthy friends requires that I be healthy as well. Usually healthy people are attracted to other people of their same level and stature. We tend to attract people at our same emotional and intellectual level. Therefore, I need to keep myself physically, mentally, emotionally, and psychologically healthy, not only to attract a higher quality of friends but for my own personal health and growth.

So since I know one of the ways my body best deals with stress is through physical activity, I have to make sure I get plenty of exercise—I have to make it a priority. I've also discovered that I need plenty of sunlight or I get seasonal depression. So each day I try to get a dose of sunlight and make sure I get plenty of vitamin D in my diet. Get regular medical checkups. It's also important to keep yourself mentally stimulated. Your work just isn't enough, and you certainly won't get intellectually stimulated watching TV. Read books and magazines, attend seminars, go on retreats—find a variety of diverse activities to keep learning and mentally stimulated. Find hobbies that allow you to relax and focus and balance your life. Deal with your emotional and psychological "issues." Figure out what makes you tick and why you do what you do. If you need counseling, seek it out.

It's important that you take care of yourself and be healthy. Sometimes that feels selfish to me. But I know from experience that if I don't take care of myself, the results aren't pretty. You can't be the kind of dad and husband your family needs if you are stressed out or unhealthy. Additionally, people generally don't want to hang around with people who are stressed out and unhealthy. You shouldn't do these things at the expense of your family, but at the expense of things you are already engaged in that are counterproductive—and don't tell me you don't have any of those in your life. If you want healthy friends—be a healthy guy.

And always remember to pray to God to bring the right people into your life. I've told this story before, but it bears repeating. When I first became a Christian, I was very lonely. I had a lot of business acquaintances but no real friends. I began praying to God every day to bring friends into my life. I did this for several years and then seemed to forget about it. As the years passed I found a large group of men at church that I went through Bible studies and home studies with, eventually going camping and hunting with them every year. Perhaps a decade later my son told me a story that brought everything full circle. He told me that his social studies teacher at high school was sharing with the class that men today do not have friends—only acquaintances. They do not have anyone they could call at 2:00 a.m. if they needed help. My son said he immediately thought, *That's not true! My dad has dozens of friends he can call at two in the morning for help.* After he told me that, it hit me—God had answered those long-ago prayers! I did have dozens of friends I could call day or night if I needed them. Do you? Do you have anyone?

4

Communicate with Your Children

Someone Is Going to Influence Them

> Every great man had someone speak a prophecy of failure over them—Satan always speaks lies early in a man's life.
>
> —Neil Kennedy

Guys, your words are heavy. They weigh a ton—just like your father's did. The words you speak to your children (and your wife) have powerful meaning and often stay in their hearts for the rest of their lives. Perhaps you had heavy, hurtful words spoken to you by a father or others when you were young. Those painful words don't go away but tend to stay burrowed in your heart and whisper in your ear when you least expect it.

Remember that your words have great power with your children. They'll remember many of your statements for years to come. Their whole outlook on life could be shaped—for better or for worse—by something you say. Whenever possible, use words intentionally to bless and to build up—whether you shout them, whisper them, or simply speak them as a normal part of the day.

One of the chief predictors of a young person's success is their perception of their parents' image of them. Speak encouragement and it builds your children up, empowering them for life. Speak negative words and it cripples the souls of your children. Unfortunately most men don't think about what they say before it comes out of their mouth. Especially when upset, we just blow off steam. Oftentimes we don't even mean what we say when we are angry.

Your words as a father spoken over your children are a prophecy of their future. Negative words are destructive, but words of encouragement bolster them throughout life in ways that border on the miraculous.

The Value of a Dad's Words

> Set a guard over my mouth, Lord; keep watch over the door of my lips.
>
> —Psalm 141:3

As a man I typically do not value words all that much. I prefer to judge people by their actions, not what they say. However, I've come to realize the absolute power my words have as a father on my children. While I try to remember how impactful my words are on my children (positively

When Men Empower Others

Over the course of 15 years, three different dads took turns destroying three critical foundations of an already sensitive little girl's worth, leaving her teetering over a bottomless pit of fear, worthlessness, shame, and insecurity. Then a 4th dad came along—even though at 17, she was beyond DONE with dads—and persisted for the next 33 years to fill that gaping hole, day after day, without flinching at her stiff arm, without tiring, without fail. Did he know she desperately needed to hear that she was loved and valued every day even though she refused to trust it? Did he know how many years it would take for the trust to build, for the words to finally sink in? Did she know how long it would take for her to let herself hope there was a father's love that would never abandon or shame or hurt her? Did he know that he was teaching her how persistent and unconditionally accepting and purely honorable the Father's love really is? Do you know my Dad? If not, I wish you could. He is a priceless gift, a God-send. I love you back, Dad.

—C. E.

or negatively), I forget from time to time. My wife just texted me this morning and encouraged me to hug our adult daughter and speak some words of love and encouragement to her. She said she has been watching our daughter listen to me speak powerful words of affirmation and love to our granddaughter and could tell it was something our daughter was yearning for in her heart. Thank goodness I have a wife who is sensitive to this or I would probably fail to speak them at all. I guess I just assume that my actions of provision, protection, and faithful commitment automatically tell my children that I love them. Unfortunately, that isn't how things work. They need to hear my words in order to internalize the things I believe about them, words that tell them that I love them, am proud of them, and believe in them.

The words spoken to children by people important to them are often taken as fact, even if they are not true. Your son probably wouldn't believe he was a garbage can no matter how many times someone told him he was one. But he might believe he was garbage if you told him he was enough times. He probably wouldn't believe other people if they told him he was stupid. But he would definitely believe he was stupid if *you* told him he was often and with sincerity no matter how intelligent he actually was.

Sometimes even when we try to say the right thing, it can be misinterpreted. One woman told me that the worst thing her father ever said to her was, "Let me show you a better way to do that." He probably thought he was teaching her a valuable lesson, but that is not how she took it. Instead, she internalized a belief that she never felt like she did anything quite right, and that led her to be performance-oriented. You can see from that example how confusing communication can be (especially between males and females—not to mention between children and adults).

As dads, one of our main roles is to give our children life advice—to teach them how to succeed in the world. Sometimes that requires us to speak words that might seem hurtful but are meant for their own good. This role often continues throughout our lifetime. Here is an experience one woman shared with me:

> I was going through a particularly rough time in my career and I was constantly talking to my father on the telephone (he and my mother live in South Korea and I live in California). I was asking him questions to help me look beyond the obvious

and see what I could do differently to be better. What was I doing wrong? It was in the middle of telling him how I was working day and night and truth be told not taking good enough care of myself physically because I was so bent on being EXCELLENT at work when he suddenly called out my name, "Cynthia. Daughter." And there was a pause.

He continued, "You are not indispensable. Those people don't care about you. If you walk outside right now and get hit by a bus, you will be replaced. They will find someone to do your job. You're doing what you're supposed to be doing. Continue to do your best. Don't let what people think affect what you know to be right. Pay them no mind and continue to do what you're doing."

In that moment it crystalized: It could have been the worst thing he ever said, but it wasn't. He wasn't being mean. I didn't take it as an insult. Instead, I realized, I am to do my best, but not at the expense of what I know to be true. It was so much "easier" to think I could change people's minds by doing something different to please them. It's much more difficult to comprehend that there are some, no matter what you do, who will not respond favorably. It's then I have to make a choice. Continue, but adjust my attitude or leave. Either way I have the power to make a choice! I learned to have a right perspective and practice in doing well, knowing that I am NOT the center of the world, ergo my job . . . it will go on without me! What a burden lifted. I eventually decided to leave. I applied for another position which would be a promotion for me. I was offered the position.

Dad, you have so much more experience in life no matter how old your children are. Don't be afraid to give them the benefit of that experience. It can mean the difference between them failing or succeeding in life. But that means you actually have to converse with them in order to impart your wisdom. Not only that, but you have to be intentional about *how* you converse with them.

Merely the tone of our voice makes a big difference in how the message is received. Words said loudly, sarcastically, or in anger are interpreted one way by children. You can use the exact same words but speak them gently or in love and they mean something entirely different. Our true inner feelings and attitude always come out in the words we speak and how we say them.

As powerful as our words are to our sons, I think they are even more powerful to our daughters. One woman is still troubled to this day by this comment from her dad: "I had just won my first pink Cadillac with three small children in tow (quite an accomplishment), and my dad asked me when I was going to get a 'real' job." That dad probably didn't intend to be hurtful. In fact, if you asked him he might say he was just concerned about his daughter and trying to help her. Nevertheless, his words left a scar on his daughter's soul.

And if you don't know by now, even innocent teasing about a girl's looks or weight can crush her for a lifetime, as evidenced by this woman: "The worst thing my dad ever said was he told me that I was so skinny that he couldn't tell my butt from my head. That comment had me developing a complex for years. But I'm over it now—sort of." That father had spoken many great words of wisdom and encouragement to his daughter, yet that one sentence is the one that rings through her mind and heart.

Never underestimate the power of your unspoken words either. Your kids (and wife) need to hear the words "I love you" at least once every day. If they don't hear those words, they won't know. Regardless of what your actions show them, if they don't hear you say that you love them, they will not believe that you do. I can't tell you how many men I've had tell me, "Well, I guess my dad loved me. He never said he did, but he must have because his actions of providing for us showed that he did." Kids who don't know if their dads love them figure maybe nobody else will ever love them either.

Better dads use their words to lift up their wives and children, never to harm them. They tell people they love them before it's too late.

Written Communication

A father's written words may be just as powerful as his spoken words. During the years when verbally communicating with our rebellious teenage daughter was difficult, I began communicating with her through notes and letters. Notes accomplish two things: First, it's virtually impossible not to read a note, card, or letter someone gives you. Second, a person will read a note all the way through (I'm not sure emails or texts are quite as effective as handwritten notes). That allows you to get your message across to them in full. When my daughter was a teen, the tone of my voice, the inflections, or maybe even my facial expressions or body language would cause her to get defensive and shut down without hearing what I had to say. In her exasperation she would roll her eyes or scowl and walk away. With notes she received the entire message and could respond after thinking it through. It appeared to be easier for *her* to communicate through notes as well. It allowed her to process the information at her own pace and choose the words she responded with carefully. This process saved a lot of arguing and slammed doors.

Here is the interesting part. She saved all the notes and letters I wrote her and still rereads many of them to this day. Those notes and cards (especially affirming ones) speak to her heart even as an adult.

Better dads use all their communication skills to connect with their children.

What Your Face and Body Are Saying When You Aren't Talking

When my children were very small, I worked away from home a lot. There were good reasons for this, but the truth is I was absent from the home for most of the days and even into the nights. When I was home, I was either sleeping or busy keeping the house running. But I thought that was okay because I assumed (as most people probably do) that babies, toddlers, and even small children need their mothers more than their fathers. I assumed that when they got older and could communicate more effectively that my role would become more pronounced and I would spend more time with them.

Interestingly, as a grandfather, I've now learned that my assumptions were wrong. Small children may indeed need their mothers to a greater degree, but if we want to be able to communicate more effectively with them as they get older, we have to spend a significant amount of time with them while they are babies and toddlers. We need to bathe them, change diapers, dress them, feed them, play with them, and read to them. These things are not just Mom's job—they are activities that develop a deep bond in the father-child relationship. And when they get older, we need to help them with their homework and teach them a multitude of other things, but mostly how to successfully live life. This is integral to the process of bonding and growing together.

Maybe that's one of the reasons it's so important for children to not only have two parents but to also have grandparents (preferably two sets) and other relatives in their lives. Grandparents provide a lifetime of wisdom, experience, and from my perspective, an innate unconditional love. Grandparents also provide wisdom and support for both parents and grandchildren. As a father I always felt under pressure to provide, to protect, and to not screw up my kids. As a grandfather I don't have those fears and stressors. I am able to relax and view my grandchild from a "bigger picture" perspective. From that perspective it's amazing to see how fantastically designed human children are. They learn to speak language from scratch within the first two years of life. They learn to crawl and walk in an even shorter period of time. The development that takes place on an almost daily basis is spectacular. I joke with my wife that if I had the time and resources (and the energy), I could create another Einstein or da Vinci out of one of these little creatures. The most important part of teaching children is learning to communicate effectively with them.

Traditional wisdom reports that up to 70 percent of what we communicate to one another is through nonverbal communication. However, that is not as cut-and-dried as we might expect. Try watching a TV show with the sound off and you'll quickly realize you have no idea what is going on just by watching the body language—certainly not 70 percent anyway. Nevertheless, a significant amount of communication is transmitted between human beings without ever speaking a word. Dr. Albert Mehrabian, author of *Silent Messages*, conducted several studies that concluded that only 7 percent of communication is through the spoken word, 38 percent by tone and inflexion of voice, and 55 percent by body language.[1]

Nonverbal communication can include facial expressions, gestures, and bodily postures, use of personal space, dress, and appearance, or variations in tone and pitch of voice. This is the process of sending and receiving wordless cues between people.

Your daughter's eye roll is a good example of a well-understood nonverbal communication. Likewise, if someone drives by you on the freeway and raises their middle finger, you know exactly what they meant without them ever saying a word. Similarly, if you come home and find your wife standing with her arms crossed, hip cocked, and tapping her foot, you can infer from her body language that she is not happy about something and can't wait to tell you about it.

The important thing about nonverbal communication is to be aware of it—both what kind of messages you are sending to others and what another person is sending you. Here are some tips to help you:

First, use good eye contact. Little or no eye contact is interpreted as if you are trying to hide something or that you are uninterested, while too much eye contact can seem confrontational or intimidating. Staring at your kids with a scowl on your face is guaranteed to frighten them, regardless of the words you speak or how you say them.

Next, be aware of the tone of your voice. Your voice can project messages ranging from excitement to boredom to anger. A man's loud voice can frighten women and children.

We might just be expressing ourselves, but they instinctively sense danger when men raise their voices.

Look for behaviors that don't match. For instance, when you ask your son how he's doing and he says, "Fine," but he is frowning and staring at the ground, you know that the words and body language do not match and need to be further investigated.

Be aware of what your body language is saying. When my kids were little, they always used to ask me if I was mad about something. I was genuinely perplexed by those questions, as I usually wasn't mad. But I guess when I am thinking about or concentrating on something, I must frown or scowl. Based on my facial expression, my kids just assumed that, regardless of what I said, I must be angry.

I had to realize that better dads learn to correctly align their body language with their words in order to communicate more effectively with their children.

Listening

In his book *Maximized Manhood*, the late great Edwin Louis Cole tells the story of a family he was counseling. The thirteen-year-old daughter had run away from home. After she returned, the parents asked Cole to talk with her. As he explored her feelings, he asked how she liked her mother. That sparked a discussion as the girl described what her mother was like. Then he asked, "How about your dad?" A sullen silence ensued and she refused to answer. As they went on to discuss other things, the girl began to tell him about a problem she had. Cole asked why she didn't tell her father. She said, "He won't listen. He never listens. When I try to explain something, he won't listen. He never takes my side of the argument, and he always blames me for everything."

Afterward, Cole brought the parents in and told them he could help them on one condition. The condition was that for the next thirty days the daughter could say anything she wanted, anytime she wanted, anyway she wanted to say it, and Dad couldn't respond—at all. The father blustered but finally agreed to try.

Three months later Cole encountered the family again. They were completely different—outgoing, happy, and unafraid to touch each other. When Cole asked what happened, the father explained that the experiment had only lasted three weeks before the daughter came to him and told him she had said everything she wanted to say and did he want to say anything back? The dad said, "As I began to listen, I realized some of the things she said were right, and that I was wrong. When she said she was finished, my wife and I just reached out and hugged and loved her. I told her how wrong I had been by being abrupt, or not listening to her side of the story.

"Then I asked my daughter to forgive me," he said. "That was the moment she began to change, and our whole family changed."[2]

Your children are trying in many different ways to get your attention every day. The noise of everyday life (TV, cell phones, computers, radios, etc.) requires us to shut some of those things out at home and be active listeners so we can hear those small, fragile voices trying to tell us what they need us to hear. Children who have their father's undivided attention feel loved and valued. Your children need you to be a good listener more often than they need you to have the "right answer." Don't be a dad with a mouth but no ears, talking but never listening. A better dad listens twice as much as he talks to his children.

Interpersonal Communication Skills

One of the great gifts you can give your children is to teach them interpersonal communication skills. These skills are essential for building and maintaining healthy relationships. Children who cannot interact and communicate well with others are very frustrated. Not being able to be understood and appreciated creates a sense of impotence and even rage. Not being able to communicate your needs to others develops frustration and eventually hostility in children.

Interpersonal communication skills are identified by employers as one of the key skills necessary to get hired for a job. These skills are crucial for tasks such as communicating with others, conflict resolution, training, and customer service.

The interpersonal skills that make up effective social interaction include listening, communicating, cooperating, negotiating, sharing, and empathizing. We know listening is important because everyone wants to be heard and understood. Communicating is making *yourself* understood, as well as exchanging ideas with others. Cooperating is working with others toward a common goal. Negotiating is resolving conflicts with others in a give-and-take process. Sharing includes others in our experiences and activities. And empathizing is understanding the needs or feelings of others.[3]

Here's how to teach your children better interpersonal communication skills. First, engage in frequent *respectful* conversations with them. Most parents spend very little time actually talking to (instead of at) their children. Most families today spend little time dialoguing with one another as a group. Stimulate dinnertime conversations of substance. Force your family to engage in dialogue and not just respond to questions with one-word answers. Next, limit the amount of TV they watch (the more they watch, the less skilled they become in dialogue). Finally, become skillful in modeling the traits of listening and negotiating in front of your children.

Better dads empathize with their children and acknowledge their successes as well as their failures in these areas.

The Power of Apologizing

I like to work challenging crossword puzzles in my spare time. It keeps my mind sharp yet allows me to relax by not thinking about anything except solving the puzzle. I've noticed that frequently the clue given for the word *err* in a puzzle is the word *sin*. But to "err" or make a mistake is not the same as to sin. You often hear politicians when they are caught stealing or having an affair say, "I made a mistake." But mistakes or errors are accidental or unintentional. To commit a sin is intentional, purposeful, and often premeditated. Someone does not accidently commit adultery or unintentionally steal money from an election fund by mistake. They do so by choice. Making a choice is not the same as having an accident or making an unintentional mistake. It's one way our society allows individuals to avoid responsibility for their actions. When you apologize and say you made a mistake when you actually made a poor choice, you are not really apologizing—you are making an excuse.

You might think I'm splitting hairs over semantics here, but words have meaning.

The greatest words or communication tool we have as fathers is to apologize and ask for forgiveness when we are wrong. This can be difficult for many men—myself included. But apologizing does not erode our authority—it actually develops respect for us from our children. Our children know when we are wrong. When we refuse to acknowledge that and repent, whether we err or sin, it makes us look overbearing, stubborn, and maybe downright ignorant.

Better dads apologize and ask for forgiveness when appropriate—even though that stings me a little just saying it.

5

Develop Your "Brand"

When Everyone Knows Your Name

> Gone is the trust to be placed in oaths; I cannot understand if the gods you swore by then no longer rule, or if men live by new standards of what is right?
>
> —Euripides, *Medea*

Every company on the planet tries to develop a "brand" for which they are known. This brand speaks volumes about the company. We all know what Microsoft or Google does just by the mention of their name. Sometimes it doesn't even take a spoken word, merely a logo—Apple's apple, the Coca-Cola symbol, and the McDonald's arches are some of the more famous. Other times a company's reputation, longevity, and/or integrity are part of their brand (Nordstrom's customer service policy comes to mind). Businesses spend billions (maybe trillions) of dollars every year trying to distinguish themselves from their competitors and establish a brand name recognition.

Each of us as individuals (and as fathers) has our own personal "brand" as well (not the kind they burn into the hide of cattle, although some people today are getting those kinds of brands). Your brand is what you are known for. It is the qualities that come to mind when people think of you. Your brand precedes you into any situation, meeting, or circumstance. It's how you deal with situations and life's struggles. Even people who do not know you personally know a little about you merely by your brand and reputation. If we are intentional about our brand, we can create one that speaks volumes to our children and future generations. If we are not intentional, we can send all sorts of negative or even destructive messages to those who look up to us.

During the summer of 2012, I was honored to be invited to attend a ceremony at the White House as part of a select group of people working with fathers around the country. We were given a tour of the White House and attended a ceremony honoring ten people in which Secretary of Education Arne Duncan and Attorney General Eric Holder both spoke and thanked us for the work we are all doing.

Making headlines a few days after our ceremony were the actions of three individuals invited to an LGBT reception at the White House. The trio of gay rights activists photographed themselves posing in front of the portrait of former president Ronald Reagan, flipping him the bird. This photo went viral on the internet.

My first thought upon seeing this picture was, "I was just standing in that very spot and it never would have entered my mind to engage in that kind of disrespectful behavior." Even when gazing at the portraits of past presidents with whom I largely disagree, the thought would never have entered my mind to be that disrespectful, especially in as an august and dignified environment as the White House. I am sure these people do not represent all of the LGBT demographic, yet I wonder about the image their actions project.

Putting aside the issue of homosexuality (which is irrelevant to this discussion), it makes me wonder about the decision-making quality, maturity, and leadership abilities of these individuals. These were not young people but appeared to be middle-aged adults, and leaders in their communities. Frankly, their behavior does not make me sympathetic to their cause or even want to sit down across a table from them and discuss their concerns. Nor would it make me comfortable in trusting their judgment or following their leadership. True leadership recognizes that our actions represent more than just ourselves or our beliefs. It also represents our families, the people who follow us and look up to us, our organizations, and even to some degree our race and ethnicity. As leaders our actions can reflect poorly on those we represent as a whole, merely by association. We've certainly seen that to be the case in the Christian community where one individual's actions reflected poorly on all Christians.

I cannot think of many (if any) issues that President Obama and I agree upon—except perhaps the importance of fathers. But I also cannot imagine myself ever committing such a disrespectful act toward him or any former president of the United States. Even more so, I cannot envision that if I ever did, I would be so immature as to photograph that action and share it with the world. How embarrassing would it be to have my family and friends see me engaging in such despicable and disrespectful behavior? What kind of example is behavior like this for our children and other young people who look up to us?

As better dads, it is our duty and obligation to exhibit healthy leadership skills through our actions, especially in today's climate of divisiveness and confusion. Always consider how your actions will affect your brand.

Trademark Yourself—With Your Wife, Plan Your Core Family Values

People want to belong to *something*, and your children are no different. They want to be associated with something honorable and bigger than themselves—something others admire. The best way to make your family an admirable entity is to develop a brand that they can be proud to be affiliated with. Too often most of us go through life reacting to whatever gets thrown at us. This is an area that as fathers we should be proactive in developing a strategy for.

Part of developing our brand is determining who we are, what things we stand for, and then some rituals and traditions we can use to reinforce and instill that brand in our children (much like companies use advertising). Nearly all great men and fathers throughout history have had a code they lived by. This code was generally focused on honor but included other ways of living that dictated how that man responded to life and the challenges it threw at him. In my book *The Power of a Man*, I include an entire chapter describing honor codes of men and cultures throughout history. I also researched the lives of twelve great Christian men throughout history and

The Importance of Family Time

"Families that devote any regular time at all—as little as thirty minutes a week with small children or thirty minutes a month with older children—to some regularly structured ritual, tradition, or activity, have children who experience much less serious difficulty than identical families in the same neighborhoods who spend no time together."[1]

highlighted the traits that were most associated with each of them in my book *A Man in the Making*. Each of these men had codes they chose to live by and many became known for those codes. For instance, Theodore Roosevelt had a very rigid code he lived by that was passed down from his father. He was known for his Olympian work ethic and strong self-discipline. Abraham Lincoln was known for his perseverance that helped him overcome so many obstacles in his life. And Robert E. Lee was known by all as having such a powerful code of honor, nobility, and integrity that even his enemies admired and respected him.

Developing rituals and traditions is extremely important for the health and well-being of your family, as well as the development of your brand. *Create a family culture that incorporates all members as being important and significant.* Research shows that kids who feel like important, contributing members of a family are much more resistant to peer pressure, cults, and outside influences than kids who don't. Kids who lack that family connection are more apt to engage in sex, drugs, and gang activities at younger ages.[2]

If you want to have a close-knit, fun-loving family, you need to be intentional about creating a positive family culture.

A culture in this sense is a group of people (a family) who have common goals and each think, feel, and act in ways that work together to achieve those goals. Your family *will* have a culture of its own—either by design or default. It will show up in the way your family solves problems, works together, and relates to one another. A family whose culture is allowed to develop by default is much like a company whose culture develops by default—the results are usually mediocre. Parents who do not think through which values they want to transmit to their children and how to pass them along often end up disappointed in the results. Developing a positive family culture takes effort and time; it doesn't just happen overnight. A family culture is predicated upon three items: values, norms, and rituals/traditions.[3]

Values are the cornerstone of your family. They are positive character traits that you and your family believe are foundational in how you live life. Our guiding family values included things like honesty, hard work, perseverance, and trust. These values were shaped by our family histories, our faith, and our education. Your values, like all families, will be different. Consider which values you believe to be most important and start working with your wife to instill them in your family culture.

Norms are rules (spoken or unspoken) about how a family behaves. They are the standards that a family uses to relate to each other and to the world. The family I grew up in believed that pettiness, arguing, and distrust were acceptable norms. My parents operated under a "do what I say, not what I do" mentality, and we didn't tell outsiders about what happened in our home. In case you were wondering—no, it's not a healthy way to raise and nurture a family.

Rituals and traditions are behaviors and routines that provide a family with a sense of purpose. They can be very simple but need to be intentional. Our rituals included dinner together as a family every night. We had minor traditions on holidays, such as watching certain movies together every year. Today our grown children still insist on watching those movies at holiday time. We also had a tradition every year on New Year's Eve of sharing our goals for the coming year. We would discuss our goals from the past year and how we rated ourselves in accomplishing them or why we didn't.

We also had family meetings whenever something important needed to be discussed. Parents most often called these, but either of the children could call one at any time if they felt it necessary. Everyone got to openly share their viewpoint (without fear of repercussions), and often a vote was taken to make a decision. Frequently, as parents we had to make the final decision, but at least the children felt significant, a part of the process, and had some amount of ownership in the outcome.

Rituals can be as simple as the ones this woman remembers:

> My dad taught me to love "good chocolate." If he received what he considered "waxy chocolate," he would take it to work and give to other people. One of my favorite memories of things I did with my dad was watching football. My dad loved the Dallas Cowboys and if I wanted the attention of my dad on a Sunday afternoon. . . . I learned the game of football and we watched it together—GREAT memories!

If you grew up in a home that did not have traditions or had unhealthy ones, take some time with your wife and think about what kind of traditions you'd like to start as a family. It's never too late to start. Make sure those traditions correlate with the values you hold to be core to your family. Those rituals will be passed down for generations of your lineage, and they are a great source of joy with your children and grandchildren. They will become the trademark for which your family is known.

Traits of Honor

If shame is the negative, honor is the positive.

—Steven Pressfield, *The Warrior Ethos*

What is your family brand? What are you known for? Your family brand will likely be the same as your personal brand. In a 1969 *Time* magazine interview, here is what actor John Wayne said he wanted his legacy to be: "I would like to be remembered, well . . . the Mexicans have a phrase, '*Feo, fuerte, y formal.*' Which means he was ugly, strong, and had dignity."[4] Not a bad heritage to leave behind, huh?

What character traits as a father do you model for your children? What kind of legacy are you intentionally passing down to your children and grandchildren? Here are a few you might want to consider in developing your brand.

One thing better dads never do is quit. Life will be hard and being a husband and father is difficult. Marriages have ups and downs and all families go through difficult spells. But even dads with no skills who stay tend to impact their children better than good fathers who leave. Kids with dads in the home do significantly better in every measurable outcome than kids with absent fathers.[5] Your presence alone is a valuable commodity in the lives of your children. Running from any problem seldom solves it—it just exacerbates the problem as it follows you through life.

Dads should be dependable and consistent. Consistency is one of the keys to better fathering. Being consistent over a long period of time models these traits. To be consistent is to be depended upon. Boys yearn to know that they can be good men. Both sons and daughters long to know what a good man is, how he acts, how he lives his life. Teach your kids that men stay. They finish the task despite any hardships or difficulties.

Other traits that better dads exhibit are sacrifice and selflessness. Most dads work hard to provide for their families. But better dads make undeclared sacrifices in the best interests of their families.

Using Memorable Sayings to Create Your Brand

Develop some memorable sayings to use with your children to reinforce the values you are teaching them. We always used to say to our young children, "Johnsons don't lie, cheat, or steal." That's pretty simple, but it instilled traits we thought were important. We used that saying both when the kids engaged in one of those actions, but also just during normal conversation at appropriate times. For instance when watching a movie and a character would lie, cheat, or steal, we would say something like, "That guy couldn't ever be a Johnson, could he? Why not?" And the kids would say in chorus, "Because Johnsons don't lie, cheat, or steal!" My kids today may not be perfect as adults, but they don't lie, cheat, or steal (at least around me anyway).

Other sayings I used were ones I had heard growing up. They often weren't as direct in the message they sent but still

Old Sayings

Rome wasn't built in a day.
The grass is always greener on the other side of the fence.
You can lead a horse to water but you can't make him drink.
An ounce of prevention is worth a pound of cure.
Beauty is in the eye of the beholder.
A person is known by the company he keeps.
If the shoe fits, wear it.
He who lives by the sword dies by it.
Never judge a book by its cover.
Two heads are better than one.
Truth is stranger than fiction.
Two wrongs don't make a right.
Honesty is the best policy.

were related to our value system. For instance, my stepfather used to talk about "not cutting a fat hog in the butt." I always took this to mean that you shouldn't get greedy. He also had a bunch of sayings that I can't repeat here.

We always told our children, "Never look a gift horse in the mouth." I'm not really sure what that means except we would use it to keep them from getting too fatheaded. We also encouraged them with some such adage similar to "Opportunities are spawned from crisis."

My friend's favorite saying with his kids was, "Experience is the best teacher, but if you can accept the information secondhand, the tuition will be a lot less."

The point is to find some really good sayings to repeat to your children. Likely your parents said some that you swore you'd never say to your kids. But of course, you will. That's okay, those are part of your legacy. Take the best of them, add some of your own, and incorporate them into the legacy you pass down to your children and grandchildren.

Actions Speak Louder Than Words

One thing we must understand is that all of our children are unique individuals. As such they must be treated differently from one another. We had a very compliant child and a very strong-willed, even rebellious child. To treat them both the same would not only have been ineffective, it would have been suicide on our part. It would also have ignored their unique gifts and skill sets. For instance, my son was very gifted academically, while my daughter was gifted athletically. If I would have had the same expectations of my daughter in school that I did for my son, she would likely have failed. Conversely, I did not have the same expectations of my son in the athletic arena as I did my daughter. He could not have met those expectations and we would have all felt like failures.

Likewise, my son was twenty months older than his sister, so in high school he got to go places, do things, and stay out later than she did. That drove her crazy, but the truth is she was not as responsible or as mature as he was at that time. She proved that over and over again by making poor choices when she was allowed to stretch beyond her boundaries. But our strong-willed child had some very strong character traits that would eventually serve her well in life. Our challenge was to keep her from self-destructing before she could get mature enough to use those traits effectively. That meant that we had to be extra aware of the example our actions modeled for her.

Our children seldom do what we say, but instead are very eager to do what we do—most especially our bad habits. Additionally, because we had a fairly public ministry, we had to be even more careful about the kind of behaviors we presented to people. Not because we wanted to present a perfect front (well, who doesn't?), but because we had a responsibility to be authentic to the people who believed in our message and benefited from our teachings. Heaven forbid that my actions would detract from a life-changing message from God that could genuinely help heal someone's family. Hence, as a family we were very aware that one's actions really do speak louder than one's words.

Traditions You Pass On to Your Children

What kind of traditions run in your family? My wife and I came from families where we didn't have any traditions, so we decided to make some. Of course, having dinner together every night was a given. But we also got a little more creative and started some of our own. We took goofy family photos over the years. I have one in my office where we are all dressed up in cowboy/saloon girl clothes (toy guns included) on a wanted poster. On another, while posing for a dress-up photo, we decided to all make funny faces at the camera. We used that as our Christmas card photo that year—everyone loved it.

A fun one was that every Thanksgiving we would watch the movie *Planes, Trains, and Automobiles* together as a family. Over the course of a week before Christmas we would also watch the movies *Home Alone*, *How the Grinch Stole Christmas*, *A Charlie Brown Christmas*, *A Christmas Story*,

Family Traditions from Readers

(1) We do two family reunions a year—one a potluck at Christmas. The second is a summer weekend at the beach. Our clan has been doing this for 40 years!
(2) We decorate the house for Christmas every year as a family, with hot cocoa and Christmas music playing. We make gingerbread houses as a family. We all gather on the couch in blankets and watch *Rudolph the Red-Nosed Reindeer*.
(3) We have a "celebrate" plate that we use for anyone who accomplishes something (report cards, star student, passes a big test, job promotion, etc.). That person gets to eat dinner on the celebrate plate and we keep a log of the celebrations. I have purchased extra celebrate plates for my kids and will give them to them each on their wedding day.
(4) We have pizza on the beach for dinner the first day of spring every year.

and culminating on Christmas Eve, *It's a Wonderful Life*. The funny thing is now that the kids are grown, they come home on holidays and insist on watching those movies together. Additionally, my wife bought a new Christmas ornament for each child every year. We now have 12,000 ornaments that I have to drag up and down out of the attic every year (don't get me started on the outside lights).

Another tradition we started was a way to do spiritual devotions. We purchased a number of books in a series called Sticky Situations. These books had hundreds of scenarios in which a child or teenager might find themselves that were uncomfortable or even downright dangerous. After each situation the book listed a number of potential ways to solve the problem—from the right answer to ridiculous responses.

Ideas for Creating Fun Traditions

- Make special events such as birthdays a big deal. You don't need a big expensive party, but make it the child's day. What do they want to do? What special meal do they want? Then have everyone sit around the table and describe what a blessing that person has been to them the past year.
- If you are of the Christian faith, make holidays like Christmas, Thanksgiving, and Easter a special time. Attend evening services as a family. Start Advent calendars, serve those less fortunate than you, take drives together to look at Christmas lights, watch football on TV (that's my favorite), have an annual touch-football game (if your family is big enough or with the neighborhood), or visit relatives every year. Other faiths have their own traditions and rituals. These are important to children because they give them grounding in a chaotic and ever-changing world.
- Take a family summer vacation every year to the same cabin or locale—make it "your" place. Try to get extended family to come every year.
- Go for walks and ice cream cones on summer evenings.

The book then listed various Bible verses that related to the best solution. We would read these around the dinner table after eating and before cleaning up. The kids would of course good-naturedly groan when I picked up the book and then shout out the most unlikely solution to each sticky situation. We would then discuss the best solution to each situation before reading a brief related verse of Scripture. This was a quick and easy way to engage them in ways that not only applied to their everyday life but that also gave them a biblical perspective of life. Today they claim to miss that dinnertime ritual even though they complained for most of the years we did it.

Even if you grew up in a home that didn't have traditions, it's never too late to develop your own. This is what it looks like in one of my friends' life:

> We didn't have traditions growing up in my family. My family moved around a lot and traditions weren't something my parents emphasized. I married a woman whose family is the opposite. This is probably why I was so attracted to her and her family.
>
> Although we have started traditions around the holidays and other special occasions, we have one tradition I enjoy more than the others. When one of our family members is involved in any activity, everyone attends—no excuses. This has helped lay a foundation of support for everyone in our family. Whether it is a weekend tennis match for Dad or an early morning swim practice for our oldest son, everyone who can physically make it there will be there. Our children have come to expect this at a young age. Not only the child who is actively a part of the event, but also the others who will only attend have come to understand that their attendance is not only required, but also needed and important. This allows them to understand how important support is throughout life. We put a high value on support and we believe this will carry over when someone is really in a position where they need emotional, physical, or any other type of support. I really believe that 95% of life is just showing up and this creates a great deal of confidence for our children just knowing we always have their backs.

Here's something that might be fun—develop a family logo. Something that tells the world what your family believes in. Then hang it on the wall in a prominent place in your home. Families throughout history have created coats of arms or family crests that were unique to their lineage. These started in Europe in the Middle Ages to introduce knights at competitions (although the Roman armies used something similar to identify specific military units). There are several sites on the internet that can help you design your own family crest. You can involve the whole family in choosing what design you want, what traits are to be included, and what colors you want used. This is a great opportunity to stimulate a lot of different conversations with your children about what your family name stands for and how you want to be remembered as a family. It then provides a great reminder to everyone as it stares down at them from the wall.

One of the really great traditions you can pass on to your kids is the tradition of staying married. That tradition has taken a severe beating the past couple of decades. But as several wise men throughout history have said, "The greatest gift a man can give his children is to love their mother." An avalanche of research has proven the significant advantages children have who come from homes where their biological parents are married and live together in the same home.

Perhaps part of the challenge to marriage today is our expectations. It seems like many people expect their spouses to meet all their needs, fulfill their every desire, and to make them whole. In other words they expect perfection. In his book *Be a Better Dad Today!*, author Gregory Slayton talks about the 50 Percent Rule. He likens this to professional baseball where no one has even come close to batting .500.

As he says, "And let's face it, we are probably lucky if we match up to 50 percent of the vision our wives had when they married us."[6] Thus, under his rule we should be grateful if our wives match up to even 50 percent of what we had hoped for.

The problem is, we have been conditioned by a culture that tells us to always seek instant self-satisfaction and self-gratification. Any unhappiness or discomfort makes us yearn for better times and seek other immediate recourse.

But all marriages (and relationships) have ups and downs. If you are struggling with your marriage, you are not alone. Most marriages go through significant challenges where one or both partners consider divorce or separation. Going through those challenges together actually builds stronger bonds and draws you closer together as a couple. Much like going through difficult circumstances (like war or a major illness) with another person bonds you tightly, the ups and downs of marriage are part of the bonding process. Going through the bad times makes the good times all that much better. People who avoid those challenges miss out on the significant pleasure that comes by going through tough times with someone and coming out the other side together.

And finally, for goodness' sake, whatever you do, spend one-on-one time with each of your children. This is the best tradition or ritual you can start bar none. Your kids crave one-on-one time with Dad. That alone time makes them feel special, important, and loved. I understand how busy most men are. It's hard to find the time—especially if you have a whole passel of kids. Not only that, but isn't doing this taking time away from your wife? Yes, you need time with your wife—no question. But my unproven theory is that the more your wife sees you authentically loving your children, the more she will love you. Not sure why—but it works. A man who attended last year's Father-Daughter Conference told me his wife said afterward, "Seeing how you now relate to our daughter makes me love you even more."

6

A Man's Spirituality

Finding Yours So You Can Teach Your Children Theirs

The wars of angels and the rage of men.

—Ben Sadler,
"You Are My Home"

Men have a complicated relationship with God. While some men (maybe the men most likely to read this book) have a strong faith and enjoy attending church, reading their Bible, and praying faithfully to God, many men do not. Their faith is not quite so cut-and-dried. Many men aren't sure exactly *what* they believe, even those who proclaim to be Christians.

It's important that we as fathers come to terms with our own faith and what we believe to be true. Because the truth is, we will pass along to our children whatever our core beliefs are, even if we don't know them.

My faith has gone through seasons as I have matured both as a man and a Christian. While I have never lost my faith and belief in the Lord, I have, as a man and father, had many questions and frustrations. I came to Christ at the age of forty—later than most men. Having lived most of my life as a nonbeliever (some would say an antagonistic unbeliever), I have a pretty good perspective on both sides of the issue. The advantage this has given me is that since my decision to accept Christ was not an emotional one made early in life (without any pressure from parents or peers), I have complete confidence in the existence of God. The challenge is that I also know my weaknesses better than most men and know in my heart that I am not any better or any worse than any other man walking the earth.

The following are some thoughts on my own faith as I wrestled and struggled through some particularly difficult times in my life. Perhaps they may be of help as you define your own faith.

The Reluctant Warrior

Church is too often irrelevant to the average guy. The pastor gives an informative—maybe even stirring (if you're lucky)—lecture on a certain passage, but seldom connects it with issues that men struggle with on a day-to-day basis. Other times the language used is superfluous or the lesson is about things that don't generally interest men, but about things that appeal to women, such as messages based around compassion, gentleness, or loving-kindness. Even more frequently, the message is performance-based, convicting men about how they fail in their everyday struggles. Especially those denominations with complicated, repetitious, and rote rituals are for the most part perceived as irrelevant for many men (even those who faithfully attend services). Many men who do go to church go to appease their wives or because it is perceived as "good for the children."

From what I have observed, what men want and need is an understanding about what the Bible teaches and how that can be applied to help them succeed in the important areas of life and then live a life of significance. They want help with the struggles—big and little—in life. Furthermore, most of the time men are not needed or embraced by the church. Men don't want to feel like they are being manipulated into being at church just to give money or serve on the elder board. Men want to accomplish something—something difficult and preferably dangerous.

Many years ago, before I became a Christian, my wife and I would take our young children to church on Sundays. While I wasn't particularly interested in Christianity, I thought the foundation was good for my children. Besides, it made my wife happy. We visited a lot of churches, but we didn't really engage much (or at least I didn't), so the churches and church members never seemed to know we were there and never seemed to care if or when we left. Of course, I'm willing to admit that my being a bit standoffish may have had something to do with their attitude.

One Sunday afternoon after several years of doing this, against my better judgment I allowed my wife to talk me into attending a picnic the church was hosting in the local park. We went and enjoyed some good food and the warmth of an infrequent sunny day in Portland.

Toward the end of the day, something happened that set my spiritual walk back at least five years. The pastor stood up and forced everyone into a circle to hold hands and sing "Kumbaya." I kid you not! It was clear by the way it was designed and staged that its intent was to trap any reluctant individuals (men) and force their participation (believe me, I frantically looked for any way to escape without being outright rude). Frankly, as a nonbelieving man, it was one of the most humiliating experiences of my life. Knowing everyone in the park was watching me and associating me with this kind of behavior was degrading. I still cringe to this day to think I was forced to participate in something that contrived and embarrassing.

Now let me say this: Is there anything wrong with holding hands and singing "Kumbaya" in a public setting? No—if that's what you want to do. But I ended up feeling trapped through this episode by what I perceived as a femininized type of Christianity (or at least a ritual of it) and it embittered my spirit toward the church and Christianity in general for many years afterward.

This pastor soon afterward ran off with the wife of a member of the church, abandoning his own wife and congregation. That also did not endear that church or the type of men in it to me at the time.

Since I'm not a pastor, this chapter will not be a theological lecture on how and why God commands you to love and lead your family spiritually. At best I struggle just like every other guy does trying to figure out my own spirituality, much less how to lead my family. But there are a few observations I've made over the years that appear to my untrained eye to be part of God's plan for a father and husband.

Why Men Matter to God

As I write this, I have been going through a year-or-so-long process of debilitating struggles. Virtually every area of my life has been ambushed. It feels like I keep getting kicked in the groin, and every time I manage to pull myself up off the ground, I get nailed again, right square in the hoo-haws. It has been one of the most difficult times of my life, especially regarding my faith. In fact, seeing the struggles I have been subject to prompted my pastor to comment that I would soon be qualified to write a companion piece to the book of Job. (Let me qualify that by saying that to date God has not allowed the lives of my children to be taken from me, and for that I am extremely grateful.)

A man's relationship with God is often a private affair. As I fight my way through my ebbing and flowing faith, I mostly feel alone, getting the normal platitudes from well-meaning friends, many of whom have never experienced the deep despair or manic highs that full-time ministry brings. Other times, some of the people who look up to me are disappointed to find I struggle with my faith from time to time. But faith without the free will to reject it is meaningless. I think God relishes my questioning him, and even being angry at him sometimes. The ability to take my faith apart and inspect its inner workings allows me to grow and intensify my relationship with God. Those with the blind obedience and vacuous smile of a sheep make me suspicious as to the depth of their faith.

The Frustration of Life

I want to share with you, very openly and honestly, some challenges that I have recently been faced with in my walk as a Christian man. To some, this may be a bit offensive. Please know that is not my intent. My intent is to reach men where they live, deep in their hearts, and hopefully encourage them through the struggles they are facing. It's been my experience that as men we all face the same struggles and challenges in life, we just seldom talk about them in a productive manner. Hopefully, this will help.

The past decade has been one of turmoil and hardship for many families, and mine has been no exception. I've chosen to be brutally honest about it in these next pages, because men who have experienced deep blows to their manhood and faith, whether they vocalize it or not, need to know they are not alone.

After spending my entire adult life diligently paying my bills on time in order to establish an excellent credit rating, I made the one financial cardinal sin that many parents commit. I cosigned a car loan and unfortunately my hard-earned credit rating was ruined as a result. At about the same time period, after owning a successful business for sixteen years, I was unjustly sued and lost my business. Rather than declare bankruptcy, I chose to pay my business debts personally instead of seeing those former faithful vendors lose their deserved accounts receivable. But that meant I now found myself surrounded by the accoutrements (a big house and mortgage, cars, debt, etc.) of an income and a lifestyle that my current employment situation in full-time ministry could no longer pay for.

To complicate matters, the economic collapse of 2008 guaranteed that I could not even take steps to solve the problem. Suddenly, for the first time in the past forty years or so, houses were no longer selling—which would have allowed me to downsize and get out from under an oppressive mortgage. And even if by some miracle they were, they were not selling for high enough values to recoup my investment and pay down my existing debt load. Additionally, jobs were not available, especially for a middle-aged man who had been self-employed for the past twenty-five years. So even though I was willing, I could not supplement my income beyond whatever God chose to allow me in order to help pay down my debt load and ease the stress of our financial burdens.

While a good case can be made that I was in the situation I was because I was not a good enough steward of the resources God had given me earlier in life, it nonetheless has been and continues to be a most frustrating experience. In fact, we went through a period of about six months that were nearly unbearable, as revenues did not allow me to pay any bills other than mortgage and utilities, except sporadically. That did not make me or anyone at the credit card, student loans, and other debtor companies very happy.

But I have learned things through these experiences that have allowed me to perhaps empathize to some degree with the struggles of my low-income brothers. I've tasted the helplessness and frustration that accompanies this man's version of poverty. However, it has also made me realize I am incapable of truly understanding the hopelessness and despair of true poverty. The frustration as a man of not being able to provide for my family in a manner that allowed me to hold my head up in self-respect was disturbingly humiliating and stripped me of dignity. The injustice of watching other men—no more deserving than me—attain money, success, and fame is galling and pushes me to be bitter and envious despite my desire not to be that way. Futility and anger surface because not being able to pay my bills on time means I am subject to constant bill collectors calling, harassing and berating me for my lack of "responsibility." The righteous indignation that comes from not being able to do things other men take for granted sets my countenance at a slow boil. And the emasculation that results from not having options to do anything about it, or worse, the skills and knowledge to change my circumstances, is humbling at best and destructive to me and others at worst.

And because of these circumstances, the "bad credit" prejudice that followed me around like a stench kept me from being able to get a bank loan or be listed on my own mortgage because of my ruined credit rating—a home *I've* paid for faithfully for twenty years. Did all that tick me off? Darn right it did. Did it make me want to strike out at others in frustration and anger? Most certainly. All of this was a serious affront to my manhood.

And yet, unlike so many men who have experienced this for their entire lives, I had a small spark of hope not yet extinguished within me. That undoubtedly is the reason I did not give up and lash out at the world, or even at God, for the injustice and rage I felt at my impotence to fulfill my basic obligations as a man. While this season has finally passed in my life, I clearly remember thinking at the time, "How much longer can I go on before that spark, and with it my faith, is finally blown out like a cheap candle in a gusty wind storm? I don't know and that frightens me. Because I meet men in prison all the time who have lost that spark and acted out of their anger. There but for the grace of God go I."

Of course, when you are under that kind of stress and pressure, especially for an extended period of time, all other issues and problems become amplified and attain more importance than they deserve. A frightening event happened to me awhile back which illustrated my growing frustration. Having grown up in a violent alcoholic home, I dealt with it by learning to inflict violence on others before they could hurt me, or at least as a first response to confrontation. After being healed by God's forgiveness, I put those angry and violent days behind me. But much like a recovering alcoholic, the intoxicating allure of my "addiction" (or programming) is always straining against its leash in the background, looking for an opportunity to pounce back into my life. I've learned to keep it under tight control through massive amounts of self-disciple and prayer. But as the pressures mounted in my life, my frustrations grew, stimulating the rage of the beast within.

While at a big-box store one day, the crowds of people were closing in on me and rubbing my nerves raw. My financial situation was weighing heavily on my mind. As I approached one busy aisle, a scrawny middle-aged man was blocking the aisle with his cart as he casually read the label on a bottle. He had the insouciance, the nonchalant air, of a typical self-absorbed Oregon liberal. Since no one could get past him in his self-centered display of indifference, I casually and politely mentioned that his cart was blocking the aisle. Without moving his cart or looking up, he sarcastically said, "Yeah, thanks." A bit confused by his attitude, I said, "Excuse me?" To which he said (still without giving me the courtesy of looking at me), "You'll get over it."

All the rage and impotence I had felt for the past six years roared up in me, and I instinctively started to lash out. I could actually see my actions in slow motion—striking him with a lightning-quick shot to the throat and, with a death grip on his larynx, flipping him backward onto the concrete floor before methodically pounding that smug look off his face. Questions roared through my head: *Who does he think he's talking to? Doesn't he know what I'm capable of doing? Who does he think* he *is anyway?*

But then, like a painfully bright speck of light in the dark red hue of my rage, I very clearly saw an image of me being led out of the store in handcuffs with bloody knuckles, and the confusion, humiliation, and tears of my wife as she was left behind with all the people in the store looking at her with recrimination because of my actions. I then saw the destruction to my career, family, and ministry because of my momentary loss of control. I knew that once that pent-up rage was released, no force on earth could have stuffed it back into its urn until the power of its violence was exhausted.

It was the hardest thing I have ever had to do in my life, but I swallowed my pride and frustration and walked away. For days afterward, though, my blood boiled as I recounted that encounter. My desire for vengeance was palpable. It throbbed through me as I repeatedly regretted not having acted to salvage my self-respect and dignity. My mood was surly and despondent. In fact, my hands shake as I write this today at the memory of my frustration and unfulfilled need for vindication and revenge. Many men with abusive fathers suffer from suppressed rage that they either learn to heal from or it destroys them and those around him.

Normally that type of scenario probably would not have bothered me, and I would have shaken off his rudeness with an indifferent shrug of my shoulders. But because of the intense pressure I had been under for not only the past six years but by the extreme magnification of that extra pressure the previous six months, I was just about willing to take another man's life with my bare hands if given the opportunity.

What does all this have to do with a man's faith? Everything! My challenge (and most other men's) is to understand God's presence in our lives and what his plan is for our lives. Because men are so performance-oriented, it is difficult to have faith when we do not see any results from our sacrifices. The frustrations of life can be overwhelming. I believe most Christian men *want* to live holy lives and have a close, personal relationship with God (whatever that means) but struggle where the rubber meets the road. Why? Because they don't see any difference in their lives. At best, their lives get calm and boring, at worst their lives are harder and more frustrating while trying to fulfill the nearly impossible-to-achieve performance-tenets of a Christian life. While that's not what a Christian life is supposed to be, we seem to have made it into that very thing.

But for me and I suspect most men, faith is what keeps me from doing things that would harm others for my own self-gratification. It gives me a moral foundation to judge my actions against, as well as the self-discipline and accountability to control my behavior. I have no doubt that given the same set of circumstances previous to coming to Christ, I would have followed through with the big-box store scenario.

All these struggles I am experiencing cause me to question whether God cares and why he does little to nothing to alleviate my circumstances on earth. Is this attitude a personal character flaw or a weakness of my faith? Probably both. And by admitting all this, I expect there might be some pastors who won't be inviting me back to speak to their men. But others understand that by being honest about our struggles and how we deal with them, we can give our men hope. I think many men in our culture are faced with these frustrations of life to one degree or another. They question whether God cares, why he doesn't show himself more, and why our prayers are so seldom answered (at least in ways we expect or can grasp). This isn't the venue to go into a long theological discussion of the ways God manifests his presence in the world and in the lives of human beings, but it is to say that most men question God's existence and struggle with the concept of having faith in something they have no control over. Because men are performance-based, they tend to shy away from believing in anything they cannot see or feel.

In his book *Pastoring Men*, Patrick Morley describes most men inside and outside the church as "friendless, has at least seen his Bathsheba, is overextended in most areas, up to his eardrums in debt, lacks meaning and purpose, feels under a lot of pressure, and is generally miserable. All of this is carefully masked behind a game face because the man knows that if the sharks smell blood, it's over."[1] He concludes with, "Most men only know God enough to be disappointed with Him."[2] Frankly, those descriptions even fit me from time to time, and I know without doubt I've seen God at work magnificently through my ministry.

And yet the very thing men need most to alleviate these life challenges is faith and the presence of God in their lives.

The Challenge of Faith

All of this had a profound effect on my spiritual walk. In fact, I confess that for several months I was at the deepest chasm spiritually I had ever been in. In my weakness and despair I was questioning my faith, my belief in God, whether God existed, whether God cared about me, and why God was allowing me to go through all of this. I was angry with God—and was letting him know about it in no uncertain terms. I believed that God had lost faith in me to do his work. I was in a funk, and frankly, I was feeling terribly sorry for myself. I was struggling with being able to pray to God or read the Bible. My wife was becoming concerned about my attitude. To make matters worse, I was speaking to groups of men about *their* faith when I was struggling with my own. I felt inadequate and like a bit of a hypocrite. God was strangely quiet, as were all other sources of encouragement.

One day my brother-in-law said something that had a profound effect on me. He said I should approach a conference I was going to speak at with the mind-set of how I could be used by God. It suddenly hit me that I had been living my life worrying only about myself and *my* circumstances. I had started my ministry work to help others, but as things got tougher and tougher, my focus had somehow shifted to my own circumstances. With this new perspective I began to look at my situation in a new light. Suddenly, I had some clarity about what God might be doing in my life. I had hope again and actually started looking forward to the challenges God placed in my path each day.

A young man I have been mentoring has been observing me throughout these challenges and the process of recovery. The other day he asked how it had affected me as a man when my earning power (which had been quite high) had dropped so low. Most men derive a large amount of their self-esteem from their ability to provide adequately for their family, and

A Man and His Faith

Practical steps to keeping your faith strong

Do these consistently even if they seem mechanical or not producing fruit. God rewards faithfulness in the small things.

Attitude – Understand the value of helping others.
Desire – Expect God to work through you to change people's lives.
Read – Read your Bible daily—even if for short moments.
Prayer – Pray daily: give thanks, pray for your wife and children, pray *with* your wife and children.
Action – Be bold and courageous. God seldom uses a parked bus. Do things outside your comfort zone so he can use you mightily.
Attend – Go to church, even if it's boring. Your kids will model your behavior in this area and you really do need to worship with other believers.

I'm no different. After thinking about it, I told him that while it *had* impacted me, I almost did not feel responsible. I explained that the physical laws of the universe dictate that effort and energy expended properly (intelligently) creates a product—a result. I had been working as hard and as smart as I was capable of and nothing of substance was being produced. That was illogical and violated the laws of physics unless something supernatural intervened. That supernatural intervention could come from only one of two sources—God or the evil one. Either way, God would use it for his purposes and my goal was to learn what I could from that lesson.

So where does all this leave a father and husband when it comes to leading his family spiritually? If you are like me and most other guys I know, your wife is probably more spiritually devout (or at least spiritually mature) than you are. My wife was a Christian long before I became a believer and seems to intuitively be more open to God and religion in general. Even though I operate a ministry and feel like I am pretty close to God most of the time, my wife spends more time in dedicated Bible study than I do, reads the Bible more often than I do, and possibly even prays more than I do. She can probably quote Scripture passages more fluently than I can, and she appears to be more deeply moved during worship service than I often am. I don't know if this means she is more holy than me, but it sure makes me question who should be leading whom spiritually in our family.

A thought struck me the other day. I feed the cat and dog the same food every day. They would likely starve to death if I did not provide for them daily. I'm like the "big manna cart in the sky." Yet, they never get tired of the same food day after day. Unlike the Israelites in Exodus, they never get tired of the same manna given to them daily by a superior being. They continue to be grateful (at least the dog does) for the food I give them regardless of the sameness or nasty odor of it.

If only I was as grateful to God as my dog is to me for the blessings I am given.

Walk Your Talk

One thing I do know for sure is that marriage and raising a family are difficult. Even the Bible says those who marry will face many troubles in life (1 Cor. 7:28).

By far the most prevalent attribute cited by the women I talk to about the topic of spirituality was authenticity. They wanted a man who walked the talk. I suspect your children desire the same thing. It's what we all want. We want to follow someone who is genuine and lives life authentically. If we want our children to be attracted to our faith, we have to model that faith by being genuine and authentic—not hypocritical. My pastor is a great guy and I love him, but he readily admits he is not perfect. I choose to follow him in part for that very reason. I can also say that has not always been the case with some of the pastors of previous churches I attended. They put up this front of being perfect and not struggling with the things that I and every other person in the congregation struggled with. They thought that imperfection was a sign of weakness. That made me not want to follow those pastors, and that same lack of authenticity makes our family not want to follow our leadership—spiritual or otherwise. Our wives and kids know we are not perfect—only *we* like to project that self-delusional image.

Admit when you don't have an answer to a spiritual question and then take action to find an answer. Share your struggles spiritually and let your family know that leaders have doubts and concerns from time to time. Most of all, let them see your faith played out in everyday situations. That kind of authenticity teaches your children a powerful lesson about faith.

Families That Pray Together Stay Together

Nothing draws us closer together with another human being than praying together does.

Take the time to learn to pray with your wife and children. Yes, this is difficult—especially with your wife. Again though, if we go on the premise that the more important something is, the more difficult it is to perform, then praying together must be really important. You need to be the one who initiates this, men. Part of your responsibility as leader in the home is one of a spiritual leader. Praying with your wife will bring you closer together in so many ways. My relation with my wife is never stronger than when we are consistently praying together.

Praying with and for your children will open up avenues of trust and respect you never thought possible. The model you give them of a dad who prays is priceless. When your kids see a dad who prays, it develops respect as they know Dad is not just calling shots on his own but is accountable to the Creator of the universe. Girls need to see that a good man prays and your sons need to see that a real man is a praying man.

And sometimes, all a man can do for his wife, children, and family is to pray for them.

The Rewards of Faith

Founding a ministry fourteen years ago and being in full-time ministry for the past ten years has given me a much different perspective of God than I had before. The challenge of relying on God's daily provision has been a growing (stretching) and highly frustrating experience. The unrelenting financial pressure has aged me (possibly matured me as well) in ways I cannot begin to describe. Frankly, much of the time it feels like God doesn't really care about me personally. If he ever does think about me, it is to occasionally flick some crumbs off his table to keep me going. I often feel alone and even abandoned in the trials of doing God's work. Where is God when I need him? Certainly I see clearly the work of other forces that are opposed to me fulfilling God's work in my life. Frankly, if I had known how difficult ministry would have been beforehand, I probably would never have started in the first place. Perhaps that's why God keeps us on a "need to know" basis with ministry work, only sharing just enough to get us started on each task that comes along. If we knew the big picture, we would get scared and run away.

Then just when I am ready to quit and give up on my ministry work, he delivers some personal and miraculous blessing for me and me alone. I am blessed magnificently in ways that I didn't even know I wanted or needed. I struggle with finances and then God sends me on a weeklong, all-expenses-paid (with additional speaking fees) speaking tour of the Virgin Islands with my wife, where we get to do things most tourists would never dream of. A wealthy businessman who read my book loans us, free of charge, his beach "mansion" every year in Florida as a getaway.

One of my wife's lifelong fantasies has been to go to Italy. I've never been able to take her. At one point I had the money saved, but my company was sued and the amount I had saved for the trip was the exact amount of the insurance deductible I was required to pay in order to be covered. Then when I least expect it, God is preparing to send the two of us on a well-paid, weeklong speaking tour of military bases in Germany. We will use that as a vehicle to take another week and pop over to Rome and Paris—places and adventures to which I probably would never have been able to treat my wife.

And the last several years God has opened the floodgates and blessed me financially far beyond what I could have ever expected. I know these are blessings from God because the sources of the revenue are so bizarre that they can only be explained by divine intervention.

Those are the magnificent blessings that God bestows upon his workers. By comparison, it makes the struggles I face seem insignificant.

The Mechanics of Faith

A young man who is a friend of mine sat with me to discuss the challenges of maintaining a man's faith and what that looks like. He was a bit discouraged on what God would have him do next with his life. One of the things I told him that I have to do is to have the self-discipline to continue doing the small things that matter even if I do not see them producing any spiritual fruit in my life. For instance, I must continue to pray to God every day, read the Bible every day, attend church every week, and pray with and for my wife every day, even (especially) when I don't feel like doing all these things. Even though sometimes this feels mechanical or unanswered, I need to continue to do these small things as part of being faithful and training myself to be prepared for when God does use me.

A good analogy is the world of sports. Athletes are required to practice a variety of small drills and skills over and over again. They often complain that there is no reason to keep doing something they already know how to do. But invariably that practice allows them to react instantly in game-time situations. The muscle memory they develop kicks in unconsciously when they need it most. They are rewarded during the game by their faithfulness to practice the small things—the game is won during practice. The harder and more precise your practice is, the better you will perform during the game. I believe God rewards our faithfulness in the small areas of worship and discipleship in the same way. When the game is on the line, our faithfulness pays off big time.

The Daily Battle

I know from experience that the average guy who is not involved in full-time ministry is seldom aware of the spiritual warfare taking place around him. It seems intensified the more you are being used by the Lord and the more reliant you become upon him. Most of us spend so much time just trying to get by that we are not aware of the spirit world around us. Only when we start becoming used by God do the spiritual attacks intensify to the point where the normal day-to-day distractions are not covering our eyes like scales. The only other time we are aware of the spiritual realm is during a crisis in our lives.

And yet that battle takes place around all men. Being created in the image of God brings special challenges and battles attached to it. Being created in that image comes with the capacity to impact the world. Jesus Christ came to earth as a man and he is still impacting the world 2,000 years later—as a model for us. As men we have the potential to change the world so much more than most of us ever realize.

Men (especially as fathers) have been given a tremendous power to influence the lives of other people. People we will never meet are being impacted by what we do or don't do right now. Future generations are being directed by our actions or inactions today. Our wives and children are looking to us to provide leadership in their lives that they cannot get anywhere else but from us. We have more influence in the lives of our families than any other person walking the face of this earth. Do we take that responsibility seriously? Many men do and the lives of people around them are blessed mightily. One of the ways we do this is by healing from our own past wounds (we will address that issue in the next chapter). But those who do not recognize the power they hold in their hands waste that gift and let those under their influence shrivel and die spiritually and sometimes emotionally and physically as well.

Better dads do know that power and use it responsibly, especially to pass their faith along to their children.

7

Your Child's Spirituality

Helping Your Children Find Their Way

> There are three things that are too amazing for me,
> four that I do not understand:
> the way of an eagle in the sky,
> the way of a snake on a rock,
> the way of a ship on the high seas,
> and the way of a man with a young woman.
>
> Proverbs 30:18–19

All children are born with a body, a soul (mind), and a spirit. They instinctively believe in things they cannot see, which is one of the challenges of being a person of faith. Faith requires us to believe in things we cannot see, touch, or prove. Whether you believe in God or not, it is hard to argue that humans are nothing more than physical beings. When people die, we can actually see their spirit leave their body. So when we strive to meet the needs of our children, we should remember they are spiritual beings as well.

Author and researcher Dr. Ken Canfield says this: "They [children] possess a spirit—have had one since birth. . . . Your children can no more decide whether to have a spiritual life than they can decide whether to be a human being. . . . The question is not *whether* your children will develop spiritually. The question is *how well* or *how poorly* this aspect of their lives will be developed."[1]

Fathers are one of the most important factors in how children develop their spirituality. Think you don't matter, Dad? Think again. Not only do fathers have the power to give life to their children through their seed, through their presence, actions, and words; they also have the power to save their children's lives. Take, for example, a woman who perhaps is poor, young, and single, who finds herself pregnant. She may terminate her pregnancy if the father is absent or does not want the child. But the same woman in the same situation will be likely to have the baby if the child's father says, "I love you, I love the child, and I want to raise it together." The father, in situations like this, often actually has the power of life or death over his unborn child.

In addition, we know from a bevy of research that a father's presence in the home is life-giving to his children on so many levels. Kids without dads are significantly more susceptible to being physically or sexually abused, living in poverty, becoming sexually active earlier, using drugs and alcohol, and committing crimes than those with fathers in the home. Additionally, there is a direct link between a child's lower educational outcomes and him or her being raised in a single-parent home. Children living with both biological parents remain in school longer and attain higher educational qualifications than children in one-parent homes. Nearly all educational outcomes (grade-point average, test scores, achievement tests, and high school/college graduation) are lower in students from single-parent homes than students from intact families.[2]

Your presence or absence in your children's lives is the biggest predictor of whether or not they will live in poverty, engage in drug and alcohol use, do well in school, or engage in criminal activities.

But even more than that, fathers are the biggest key to whether or not children develop faith. A large study conducted by the Swiss government revealed some startling facts regarding generational transmission of faith and religious values:

1. If both father and mother attend church regularly, 33 percent of their children will end up as regular churchgoers, and 41 percent will end up attending irregularly.
2. If the father is irregular and the mother regular, only 3 percent of the children will subsequently become regulars themselves, while a further 59 percent will become irregulars.
3. If the father is non-practicing and the mother regular, only 2 percent of children will become regular worshipers, and 37 percent will attend irregularly.
4. If the father attends regularly and the mother irregularly or not at all, between 38 to 44 percent of children become regular attendees.[3]

This is not to suggest that Mom is not important in the spiritual development of children, but perhaps that children take cues about domestic life from their mothers and conceptions of the outside world from their fathers. It appears that if Dad takes God seriously, then his children do as well.[4]

Whether you want the job or not, whether you feel qualified or not—Dad, you *are* the theology professor in your home. You set the spiritual tone and foundation in your home and likely the belief system your children adopt—at least until they are old enough to develop their own, which they will have to eventually. Every day you are teaching your kids about God, faith, truth, and the Bible through your actions and words. Didn't think you were signing up for that when you decided to become a father, did you? And unfortunately for you, once you are in this position, you can't resign.[5] Because even your resignation will teach your kids something about faith. And being passive or apathetic about your spiritual walk teaches them even more.

The majority of dads feel that leading their family spiritually is one of the most challenging tasks they face. When I came to Christ at forty years of age, I definitely felt that being the spiritual leader in our home was going to be a challenge. My kids were eight and ten years old at that time. So how can we best go about being the spiritual leader that our children need and that God has called us to be? We have to start by refining our own spirituality so that we can pass it along to others. This often begins by healing our own spiritual wounds.

Healing Your Wounds First

As grown men, we should never underestimate the power of our past to dictate the kind of men we are today. Several years ago I started taking acting classes to improve my speaking and stage presence. Little did I know that an exercise in class would lead me to uncover some startling emotional epiphanies, as illustrated by the following story:

> There was once a young boy who was raised in an alcoholic home—both his mother and stepfather were alcoholics. Despite being under the impression for most of his early childhood that this lifestyle was "normal," he eventually found the stress and pressure of trying to be "perfect" in order to appease his parents' unrealistic and unreasonable demands to be too much to endure. He couldn't make them happy no matter how much he tried and that was frightening. Frightening because it was a very violent environment—physically, emotionally, and ever increasingly psychologically dangerous.
>
> The boy could clearly remember a day when he was about ten years old when he first knew that the boy he was could not survive in this environment. Until then he had been quite confident that, as a person, he was created wonderfully—a nice, compassionate, and intelligent boy who innately believed that his life was destined for greatness in some form or another. It was a good and secure feeling. But one day the boy suddenly realized he was being forced to kill that boy. Instinctively he knew that nice boy could not endure the abuse, and if he was to survive, that naive, thoughtful, and kind-hearted boy had to go or he would be destroyed and cease to exist altogether. To protect himself, that good boy had to disappear. That's when he first made the decision to kill that boy.
>
> As the oldest child, he had the expectations of an adult placed upon him. His resentment and rebellion to this unfair burden resulted in him filling the role of the "bad guy" of the family, causing him to believe untruths about himself even as an adult. He was told lies that fueled his anger: "It's

> your fault—you don't fit in. You think you're better than us. Who do you think you are anyway? You'll never amount to anything!"
>
> For years afterward, the young man silently cried tears of frustration, sadness, and most of all anger for the loss of that innocent boy. From that day forward he was angry. His anger acted as a shield to protect him from the onslaught of the demons raging against him.
>
> The boy stuffed his grief and mourning over the loss of that young boy and the "man he could have become" deep inside where no one could find it (including himself). As he grew into a man, that boy was forgotten and replaced by the "survivor," and he eventually became the kind of man he did not like or even want to be. Life was difficult and frustrating. Anger and pain were constant companions.

As you probably guessed, both those boys were me—murderer and victim.

The work required in the acting classes to "get in touch with my emotions" shocked me into remembering this little boy from my past. My heart cries today for that boy/man and what he could have been. But even more so, I cry because that man I became possibly (in some way) harmed the soul of the woman my wife could have been, as well as the potential in the precious souls of my children. May God forgive me.

But here's the good news: God *has* forgiven me—for all my sins. Not only that, but his forgiveness and unconditional love have allowed me to begin my own healing process. I have since discovered that the first little boy is not dead—he was merely locked behind a prison door. Once that dungeon was flung open, his light has been shining bright for the world to see! As I grow emotionally as a man, I am learning to be driven more by my heart and not so much by just my intellect. I've realized that my intellect was a "survival of the fittest" programming designed to protect me, and that I did the best I could as a husband and father. But best of all, my wife and children graciously forgive me as they realize I was placed in their lives as part of the experiences God gives people on their own journey in life. As I continue to grow and evolve emotionally as a man, I look forward to the day when I become the man God once envisioned me to be even before I was born, instead of the man I was forced to become by wounded people who got comfort by wounding others.

If you've endured trauma as a child, I encourage you to seek professional healing—it's difficult but worth the effort. I spent too many years unaware of who I really was and becoming someone I did not want to be.

Interestingly, as a side note to this story, for the past several years as a middle-aged man I have had a recurring nightmare that I never understood until now. It involves me as an adult being forced to fight for my life against a diabolical serial killer. Instinctively I know that serial killer is me—a doppelganger if you will. What is so frightening about this dream is I am outmatched—the serial killer is smarter and more ruthless than I am and so has a big advantage. I generally awake sweating and fearful just before I am killed, but knowing it is just a matter of time. Today I now understand where that dream comes from as the two "boys" within me struggle with each other for control. The "survivor" is more cunning and resourceful, but the naive boy has good on his side.

It's difficult to help anyone else with their problems until we have first solved our own issues. I know too many people who only accept advice from people either in the same predicament as theirs or in worse situations, rather than accept advice from someone who is where they want to be in life. This is illogical but very prevalent. If you want to own a successful business, should you ask someone who has started and operated one or more successful businesses or someone who has never owned one? If you want a good marriage, should you talk to people who have been successfully married for several decades or take advice from someone who has been divorced three or four times? (I guess if you want to know what *not* to do in a marriage, the latter might be a reliable source.) Same goes with raising children. With that strategy in mind, find dads who have raised or are raising good, spiritually strong kids to emulate and get advice from them rather than from some poor schumck who has abandoned his family or whose kids hate him.

Our problems and wounds affect our spirituality and the relationship we have with God. Unfortunately, healing our own wounds is hard work. Like most everything in life that is worth something, it is difficult. Not only that, but we have forces actively working against us, trying to prevent us from succeeding. As Christians we understand this to be spiritual warfare, but even nonbelievers know there is a force that is opposing their success. As fathers, because of the invaluable role we play in the lives of our children, even stronger forces are aligned against us, anticipating and precipitating our failure. Regardless of our belief system, there are forces at work in the universe trying to keep us from succeeding in everything we do in life.

In *The War of Art*, author Steven Pressfield calls this force the "Resistance." He describes the Resistance and its effect this way:

> In other words, any act that rejects immediate gratification in favor of long-term growth, health, or integrity. Or, expressed another way, any act that derives from our highest nature instead of our lower. Any of these will elicit Resistance. . . .
>
> The more important a call or action is to our soul's evolution, the more Resistance we will feel toward pursuing it. . . .
>
> The danger is greatest when the finish line is in sight. At this point, Resistance knows we're about to beat it. It hits the panic button. It marshals one last assault and slams us with everything it's got.[6]

Have you ever had a difficult time getting started on or, even worse, finishing a project that was very important to your career? (The deadline for this very book is looming over my neck like a guillotine.) Or procrastinated doing something that was good for your health, like scheduling a doctor's appointment or seeing a counselor to help with your anger issue? The inertia of mediocrity makes it hard to do great things.

The problem is it is difficult to heal or to change programmed habits and decisions. But if we don't make the effort, we tend to pass those same wounds and unhealthy habits down to our children, and it forms one more link on the generational cycle chain. Those traits then tend to influence our children's spiritual walk as well. But we can't fix ourselves or heal our wounds by ourselves. We need help to mend wounds that we are not even aware of or change our decision-making process to one we've never had modeled for us before.

I recently came to the realization that I must have a sugar addiction. If you don't think there is an external force working against me as I try to stop drinking my favorite cola, you better think again.

Better dads seek healing for their wounds (especially spiritual ones) so that they can lead their family in healthy spirituality.

Find Your Child's "Way" or Gifting. Then Nurture It.

> Train up a child in the way he should go [and in keeping with his individual gift or bent], and when he is old he will not depart from it.
>
> —Proverbs 22:6 AMP

The verses from Proverbs that began this chapter talk about the "way" of amazing things in life. The "way" in Hebrew actually means "gifting." It is the way God has made you—the gifts he has endowed you or other living creatures with. One of the jobs of fathers is to study their children and determine their "bent" or the *way* they are wired so we can determine how best to encourage and nurture those gifts to amplify God's gift.

Each of our children is created uniquely by God. They each have strengths and weaknesses. If you have more than one child, you probably know that each one is completely different than his or her siblings. One child might be outgoing while the other is more introverted. One is athletic while the other is more interested in books and microscopes. One child can sing like a bird while the other sounds like a drowning cat. One is neat and orderly, the other is messy and disorganized. One is loud and raucous, the other quiet as a church mouse.

The verse quoted above (Prov. 22:6) is advice that Solomon gave to parents. It's not a guarantee of anything, nor is it a prediction. The key word of this verse is also the word "way," or the way they are wired and the temperament God has given them. Each of your children also has different spiritual gifts that God wants to use in their life. Psalm 139 confirms their uniqueness by saying that each person is "fearfully and wonderfully made" (v. 14).

Your goal as a father is to determine each child's bent and then help nurture them to be best able to use the gifts that God has given them to fulfill their path in life. Because each child is unique, how we train each one must be unique as well. Because their bent and role in life are each different, they each require different training. A German shepherd being trained as a police dog would be trained very differently than a Lab being trained as a guide dog for the blind or a springer being trained as a bird dog. Same with our children: while we must have a spiritual foundation that we rely on and base decisions against, we also have to train each child according to their unique bent. We need to find ways to relate to each child and the best teaching method for each.

One of the things that we tried to do with our kids was to nurture their strengths instead of focusing on their weaknesses. Many fathers (again because we tend to be performance-oriented) tend to focus on their children's weaknesses, not their strengths. For instance, we all have heard of the child who gets all A's on his report card along with one C. Of course the dad focuses on the C instead of all the wonderful A's his son got. But as a basketball coach I always used to tell my players, "Let's forget about your weaknesses and focus on your strengths." Your children's strengths are what will help them succeed in life, as suggested in a study of the relationship between personal strengths and confidence:

> People lean on these beliefs and habits to justify converting weaknesses to strengths, and that's a critical mistake. Gallup's forty-year, nine-million-person research on strengths shows that people are six times more likely to be engaged at work, productive, and happy when less time is devoted to fixing weaknesses and more time to building strengths. "You have development needs—areas where you need to grow, areas where you need to get better," writes strengths expert Marcus Buckingham. "But for you, as for all of us, you will learn the most, grow the most, and develop the most in your areas of greatest strength."[7]

So while our daughter was very athletic while growing up (which made it easy for me to nurture her strengths), our son was not necessarily gifted in those areas. We had to find things he was good at and nurture those in order to grow him in the way of his bent. We encouraged him to join the school band in middle school. He ended up playing the saxophone and several other instruments all through high school and into college. He played in the concert band, orchestra, the pep band, and the jazz band, and even played in some clubs. It helped him succeed at something which in turn gave him a healthy self-esteem. If I had tried to force him to play sports, it would not have been as nurturing an experience for him.

It worked the same way spiritually. Our daughter was not particularly interested in sermons, reading the Bible, or small group studies like our son was. She was, though, very interested in learning about the way of God through serving others less fortunate than her. So she readily walked with us at prayer vigils outside abortion clinics, served in soup kitchens, and worked with developmentally disabled children. We also always had her working with the children our ministry was involved with, whether it was through the child care for workshops and seminars, kids at our single moms' family camps, or speaking with me at father-daughter conferences. She also volunteered (then worked at) a horse ranch providing therapy for disabled and special needs children and adults.

Today, as an adult, she has her own business providing individual and group exercise and socialization programs for developmentally delayed children and young adults. In addition, she works for a large federal grant fatherhood program, managing the child care program—which is quite large. Despite being pretty rebellious as a teenager and showing no signs of wanting a walk with God, her faith today (much to my surprise) is very strong and growing because of her life experiences.

Likewise, my son was involved in our ministry programs as well as a variety of service projects through the Boy Scouts and church, which have developed a very compassionate heart for others within him. His path led him through a different way of finding his own faith, which, similar to my own, was more of an intellectual experience.

The Greatest Gift

One of the functions of faith and religion is to remind people that they are not God. It is through the process of acknowledging and worshiping an omnipotent being greater than you that humility, faith, and strength of character are developed. That's healthy for a variety of reasons, not the least of which is that it keeps us from believing we are our own God. Not only that, but recognizing and worshiping a holy God helps keep kids from becoming self-focused. Little children already seem to know about God. They are in awe of all they see and recognize a certain spiritual element in the world that adults seem to miss.

Prayer is one of the best things you can do as the father of your children. It is also one of the best virtues you can teach your kids. A father's prayers for his children may carry weight with the Lord as it speaks to his heavenly Father heart (James 5:16). When your children see you intimately praying, it instills in them the belief that Dad does not think *he* is God. They are more likely to take your instruction and advice with more credibility because they recognize that you are accountable to someone important—the Creator of the universe.

Here's one dad who understands how to instill and develop spirituality in his children:

> I have also created a small tradition with my children when I tuck them into bed in the evening. After we say our prayers together, I look at them and I put my hand on their heart. I tell them, "God has very big plans for you." I know they don't understand quite yet what this means, but I am trying to instill in them that their life is of great importance and they should feel as if God has great expectations for their lives. My three-year-old daughter now responds with, "I am little, Daddy, God has little plans for me." I tell her, "No, Liza, God has big plans for you." The other night she asked me, "How am I going to carry those big plans?" I told her I would carry them for her until she grew big enough to carry them herself. She agreed.

Teaching your children to pray is easy. First, dads, just model it for them. Pray out loud at meals and pray over your kids at bedtime (a very powerful experience). Kids need to

Steps of Prayer

Consider using these steps when teaching children to pray:

- Start by acknowledging God with "Our Father in heaven . . ." or a similar sacred greeting.
- Confess your sins (help your child with this concept).
- Express gratitude for what you have by saying, "Thank you for . . ."
- Ask for what you need: "We/I ask you for . . ."
- If you are Christian, end with "In the name of Jesus Christ. Amen."

learn to pray because the belief in an omnipotent, benevolent God can assuage many of life's fears for a child, especially during scary times.

I think sometimes we get too hung up on using fancy, stilted wording when praying. Sometimes prayers are mechanical, repetitive, and filled with obscure language. But that's not how I pray inside my head when I'm talking to God. Teach your kids to talk with God just like they would carry on a conversation with anyone else. But there are some things that are probably helpful for kids to learn while praying.

Teach your children to pray for protection. When bad things happen in the world, kids are afraid that something will happen to them as well. Just asking God to keep them safe can do a lot to relieve their fears. Teach them to pray for others who are in need. This not only teaches them to petition God during times of trial, but also teaches them compassion and empathy for others. Most of all, teach them to express gratitude when they pray. This makes them conscious of their blessings. It also keeps them from having an entitlement mentality and helps stop them from becoming little narcissists.[8] And of course, the greatest thing we can do for our children is to pray *for* them.

Dad—even though it may *seem* difficult, it really doesn't take much to begin to be the spiritual leader in your home. Your wife and children *want* to follow you (sometimes desperately so). The most common plea I hear from wives is, "I wish my husband would lead our family spiritually." All you need do is start taking some baby steps and they will fall in line behind you. Your children are looking to you for leadership with this mysterious entity called God. They learn their faith from one of two sources: you and Mom, or the outside world. The least you can do is make sure you actually know what your faith is, then help them understand what that faith means and looks like.

Better dads make the effort to lead their families spiritually, even if they don't feel qualified.

8

Teaching Character

Allowing Your Children to Suffer

> Losing all and reclaiming it again while friends keep a suspicious distance and the words of critics sear the soul—these seem to me about the hardest things a man can face, and it is not surprising that many men never recover themselves.
>
> —Stephen Mansfield

Suffering and overcoming challenges are key components in creating good and great men. (I would further say that overcoming obstacles and difficulties also creates powerful character qualities in females as well.) This is important because being a good father is not so much about being a good parent as it is about being a good man. Many men know a lot about the subject of parenting, but they may not be very good men so they tend to not be very good fathers. Conversely, some men don't know anything about the topic of parenting, yet they are good men and so, more often than not, tend to be really good fathers.

Does that make you feel better? It did me. When I first discovered that concept, I felt like a huge pressure was lifted off my back. Being a good parent was something I didn't know much about, and frankly it was a bit intimidating. But I could be a good man—at least I could try. Knowing that even if I didn't know much about parenting, I could still be a good father just by being a good man was very liberating.

Fatherhood and manhood seem to be intertwined, for good or bad. The character traits of the man transfer to the father, and those of the father transfer to his children. That said, if we want to raise children to become honorable, courageous, compassionate, and loving adults, we have to be those things as their fathers.

Unfortunately, our culture no longer values shame or honor—two traits necessary to create good character. That's because shame and honor imply moral judgment. Without the will to judge right or wrong, we can never be honorable. Without the ability to feel shame, we can never develop character traits such as compassion, honor, and integrity. Those who do not feel shame cannot suffer, and those who do not suffer cannot develop character.

Better dads help their children develop character.

Suffering Creates Character, Trauma Does Not—What's the Difference?

> All daring and courage, all iron endurance of misfortune make for a finer and nobler type of manhood.
>
> —Theodore Roosevelt

This past year my wife and I have found ourselves in a circumstance where we are, at least temporarily, raising our two-year-old granddaughter. We've had her almost a year now. If you've ever been around a toddler, you know how much energy they take and how much attention they require. It was quite a culture shock for us to go from empty nesters to suddenly and unexpectedly raising a baby.

It dawned on me the other day that one of the challenges of this situation (of which there are many) is that my wife has reverted to "mother mode," and so I seldom get her undivided attention anymore. When our kids were teens or had grown and moved away, they didn't need her as much, and so I was the center of her universe and she paid rapt attention to everything I said (and frankly whatever my needs were as well). I didn't realize it at the time, but it was quite exhilarating—it was just like the early days of our marriage! Now she has to devote so much of her attention to "The Squirt" that I seldom get more than a small piece of her consciousness. That dynamic was probably in place when our children were little, but I was likely working a lot and didn't realize it as poignantly. The truth is, I probably didn't like it then and I certainly don't like it much now. I understand the necessity, but I still don't care for the results. As a father/grandfather that sounds a bit selfish, but as a man/husband I think you guys know what I'm talking about.

My point is that life is difficult, and it doesn't seem to care about my needs or wants most of the time. Also, it never seems to get any easier no matter how much older and experienced you get. Life still presents challenges. The good part is that those challenges are what develop our character and teach us to be the kind of people who can make a difference in the world.

Greatness is not possible without some sort of failure to overcome. Suffering develops character. Without suffering we never have the opportunity to test ourselves and see what we are made of.

If that's true, then it goes without saying that our children need to suffer in order to develop a healthy character. For so many of us, the challenge is, how do we allow our children to suffer enough to develop character without traumatizing them? Many parents today rescue their kids too often, never allowing them to face the consequences of any of the choices they make. "Helicopter" parents hover over their children, never allowing them to take healthy risks and possibly get hurt. Since it's virtually impossible to succeed at life without taking some risks, these children are psychologically crippled by the very thing their parents think is helping them.

Upon reflection, my wife and I readily agree that we rescued our children too much while they were growing up. With both of us having come from abusive and highly dysfunctional backgrounds, we wanted to spare our children the agony of growing up under those kinds of circumstances. But by not allowing them to suffer through their failures, we kept them from fully developing key character traits that would have benefited them greatly throughout their lives.

Experiential Learning—Experience Is the Best Teacher

> There comes into the life of every man a task for which he and he alone is uniquely suited. What a shame if that moment finds him either unwilling or unprepared for that which would become his finest hour.
>
> —Winston Churchill

How do you think an authentic man—or a better dad—should respond to loss or devastation? It's a lesson you are teaching your kids every time something challenging happens in your life. Are you a rock they can depend upon? Or do you fall to pieces every time something out of the ordinary happens? Or worse, do you shut down or quit?

Most people are afraid to try something new for fear of failing or looking like a fool—especially as they get older. The fear of humiliation prevents them from trying something that might turn out to be their greatest gift in life. And so this stops many men from even trying to lead their families spiritually or even domestically.

I always tried to instill in my kids the notion that the only time you fail is when you don't try. The truth is, everything I've accomplished in life I literally bluffed my way through until I figured it out. Every job I was ever hired for I fudged on my experience in that industry and position. I then faked it until I could learn the skills needed to succeed at that job. Every business I started, I'd never done that type of work before (nor had I owned and operated a business). I'd never written a book before I wrote the first one (talk about faking it). And of course when you are a first-time father without having had a positive role model to learn from while growing up, you are faking it every step of the way.

So it is with all of us. I told my son when he was a teenager that he shouldn't be afraid of asking the beautiful and popular girls out on dates. *Someone* dates those girls and eventually marries them. He had as good a shot as any young man, but only if he took the risk (coincidently a lot of beautiful women tell me they had trouble dating because everyone was afraid to ask them out). When either of my kids were looking for a job, they were quick to dismiss any job with which they had no experience. But most of the time, businesses hire someone hoping they can get a good person of character with no experience (at least on entry-level jobs) so they can train them their way with none of the bad habits fostered in other jobs.

The truth is, whenever anyone begins anything—whether career, relationship, or even life—they do so not knowing how to do it. Being bad at something is the beginning of becoming good at it. Hard work and a good attitude count for much in life. Most of life learning is on-the-job training. Having a loving parent(s) to help teach some of these life skills is a huge advantage in life.

I believe kids today need an inoculation against evil that can come from adult advice, but may be better learned by personal experience. I'm not advocating that kids go get into trouble just to learn that it's not a good idea. On the other hand, if they only have rules that someone else sets down for them, I've seen that it frequently misses the mark in personal adoption. As fathers we have to resist the temptation of creating too many rules that keep our children from learning through experiences. Oftentimes, especially in the church, we think this is a good strategy—that we are producing children who obey and toe the line. But by not allowing them to learn from the errors of life experiences, they are not equipped to deal with real-life situations.

My friend tells the story of good intentions gone bad:

> A Christian family who are friends of ours had many non-negotiables in their home for their kids growing up. Everything from what radio station they listened to, to who they could play with and when. At the time I thought this could

> be a problem. These are good people! I co-led a youth group at church with the mom, and Dad's a solid man. Doing the right thing, they believed, was wrapping the kids up pretty tight with rules—but few liberties. Very sadly, when their oldest daughter became an adult, she did what she felt was her duty by taking in two drug babies, one with the syndrome where he eats everything (don't remember the name for it). I didn't know how she could deal with such responsibility as she'd never had to face the world's trouble. Very sadly she ended up unable to cope and killed the little boy by shaking him to death. She spent time in prison and her life spiraled down thereafter. I've wondered if she had been exposed to situations growing up where she had to make a decision for herself, not just doing what someone else said to do, would she have developed the wisdom to make different choices?

Don't get me wrong, I'm not advocating permissiveness, as children do need structure and values presented to them that they can one day adopt for themselves. But I'll do whatever I can to help them figure this out for themselves. I think that's the way God tends to deal with us—we have lots of rope to hang ourselves and he loves us in spite of us. If he can put up with me, I can put up with a little independence in my kids, who I hope will learn the right balance of putting up with their kids' independence too. I think that's what makes us stronger, like resistance or weight training. If you've never engaged in the sweat and ache, you're probably not getting a whole lot stronger.

Perhaps the greatest skill we can teach our children comes by letting them fail—and then allow them the privilege of suffering the consequences of that failure. Every success comes from failure. Those who never fail are those who never try anything. Teach your children that the way to succeed in life is to try something, fail, get back up, and persevere until they succeed. That's how we learn best, how we develop a healthy self-esteem, and how we succeed in life.

Better dads know that and embrace their children's failures, using them as teaching experiences. I'm not going to say better dads want their kids to suffer, but they do allow them to learn how to live life by learning through their failings. Then they are there to help them get back up again, dust them off, encourage them, and send them (sometimes push them) back in the ring again.

Teaching Your Children to Learn from Others

Human beings have a strong instinct for self-preservation. We like to take the easy, comfortable road. This applies to not only our fear of death or physical harm but also psychological failure or emotional wounding. Unfortunately, relationships are fraught with the potential for both pain and heartache. As fathers we must overcome that natural impulse to avoid anything difficult or unpleasant—if for no other reason than our actions are teaching our children how to live life. By modeling courage and perseverance in the face of adversity, we teach our children not only that this is how men and fathers act, but that is the way *they* should live their lives as well.

Attitude is the key to everything in life. A negative, disrespectful attitude creates barriers in all areas of life, be it learning, relationships, or success, while a positive, respectful attitude allows us to overcome any barrier no matter how egregious, develop healthy relationships, and live a happy, contented life.

Ask your children who they look up to and what they admire about those people. Help them identify what character traits they like in their heroes. If we never identify what character traits we admire, how can we expect to internalize them? Use admirable family members, friends, or even strangers as examples to learn from. We can even find some great role models (positive or negative) in movies and TV programs. Frankly, we can often learn as much from negative examples as we can from positive ones.

While a mother and father are the two biggest influences in a child's life, it is important that other people help to reinforce your values and teach children things they need to know in life. These are things that the children may even be resistant to learning from the parents but more easily accept from another person—sometimes even a stranger.

I spent quite a few years telling my son that he needed to start saving money. Then one day a teacher he looked up to in school made a comment about the power of compound interest. It was like the cogs in my son's internal mental clock clicked forward another gear and everything suddenly aligned and became clear, making sense for the first time in his life. You'd have thought it was the only time in his life he'd ever heard that sentiment stated. Not only that, but the teacher was obviously the most brilliant man in the world. Over the years, when my children came to me with some great insight, I've found myself thinking, *But I've been telling you that for years*.

Precisely because of things like that, I've become more convinced than ever of the importance of grandparents, aunts and uncles, cousins, and other extended family in a child's life. Not only do they provide a sounding board for children, they are also allies in reinforcing key values that the parents believe in strongly, which provides a solid foundation for the child. Grandparents, aunts, and uncles can also offer explanations, interpretations, and other ways of looking at topics and decisions that parents make, which can help the child understand the situation better. Plus they can be there to encourage your children to take risks and catch them when they fall.

Many times your children will talk to other adults who have invested in their lives about topics they would never discuss with their parents. When children believe multiple people love them, they feel better about themselves and realize they can depend on people besides their parents to help and care for them. It provides children a more varied and diverse group of resources with life experience to get information and wisdom from. It's important for children to have intimate relationships with more people than just their parents.

One of my great regrets in raising our children was that I did not pull up stakes and move from Oregon to Southern California to be around my biological dad and my siblings. I used the excuse that I owned a business, but in hindsight I could have started a new business down there and been just as or even more successful. It was lack of confidence and dim foresight on my part that kept me from making that choice. Instead we raised our children by ourselves with no support system. A better dad would have made the decision to move for the benefit of his children.

But we did want our children to be around and be influenced by people in various settings. My son was in scouting from Cub Scouts up to Eagle Scout. He gained tremendous knowledge from the adults he was surrounded by in the Boy Scouts. Both my son and daughter were involved in church youth group for many years, as well as sports, debate, student government, band, and a variety of other activities where they were exposed to knowledgeable people with good intentions for their lives. We also had a plethora of friends over the years who cared about their well-being and spoke into their lives.

If your children are fortunate enough to have extended family in their lives, I encourage you to find ways to allow them to spend time together. Even if they live long distances away, I think the value the children will get from those relationships are well worth whatever cost and difficulties it may entail. For whatever reason, I seem to know a lot of people who harbor resentment against their parents and so do not let their children spend time with them. I understand that if you had bad experiences growing up, you (or your wife) might think, "They weren't such great parents to me. Why should I allow them a chance to mess up my kids?" The truth is many people who were poor parents end up being excellent grandparents. Obviously, if your parents were abusive, you have to make sure to protect your children and keep them safe. But if you are using your children to get even with your parents, you are hurting your children as much or more than you are your parents. If your parents actually *want* to be grandparents (which some don't), I encourage you to allow them to cultivate a relationship with your children. You might just be surprised how well it works out. Besides, if you're like I was, you can use all the time alone with your wife you can get.

Finding Hope in Your Child's Suffering

Suffering teaches character, and yet for most parents it is unthinkable that they should allow their children to experience any form of suffering. Many young people today have never suffered a day in their lives, and so some (even those from the best families) feel lost, unnecessary, or insignificant. This can create a host of problems for a young person.

Human beings need to be needed. This is such a strong need that if people feel that their life is insignificant or has no purpose, they may commit suicide. They might also behave in ways that give them a false sense of belonging or importance. They might seek undue attention, use their power harmfully (bullying), or seek revenge for perceived slights or wrongs. Rebellion or passive resignation are linked to this kind of perception of oneself. In young people these feelings can result in destructive behaviors like drug and alcohol abuse, promiscuity, or criminal activities. Studies of the chemistry of the brain show that the chemicals that regulate mood, motivation, resistance to illness, and depression are highly influenced by our perception of personal significance.[1]

Children need to struggle. If for no other reason than that persevering through our struggles matures us and develops healthy self-esteem. It helps us to feel valuable and important. They need to wrestle with questions and problems. They don't need to be rescued and seldom want to be told all the answers. But they do want to be valued.

Teach your children to learn how to suffer—to suffer well. Suffering is a fact of life—no one escapes this world without suffering. Those who use that suffering to learn and grow from are much healthier and happier than those who wallow in their despair. Here are four tips to help them through their journey:

1. Use Christ as an example. As the ultimate example of someone who suffered, we should look to him to see how he persevered through his circumstances. Study Christ

(and Job as well) to see how he dealt with suffering. You'll find that he dealt with it mostly by praying for God's will.

2. Understand that suffering is part of life (just like death) and no one escapes from its unpleasantness. Therefore if it is something that everyone who ever has or ever will live has faced, perhaps it should be looked at as a positive instead of a negative circumstance. Jesus's brother James says this of struggles and trials: "Consider it pure joy, my brothers and sisters, whenever you face trials of many kinds, because you know that the testing of your faith produces perseverance. Let perseverance finish its work so that you may be mature and complete, not lacking anything" (James 1:2–4 NIV).
3. Understand that suffering develops character traits such as endurance, hope, and faith, which allow us to live lives of significance.
4. Teach your children to make sacrifices for the sake of other people. Suffering for others makes us able to suffer well. Not only does this allow us to live a life of significance, it makes the world a better place. And in the doing, it makes us (and our children) more Christlike.

We think we have eighteen years to teach our children a moral foundation, but that's not true. In reality we only have a few years. At best, by the time our children are tweens they pretty much have the character platform set in place that they will have for the rest of their life. We don't have a lot of time to waste. As difficult as it may be, it's better for them to suffer a little under your guidance when children than to suffer the much greater consequences as an adult because they didn't learn how to suffer well.

Why Your Children Need a Dad's Strength

> The simple willingness to fight back after misfortune is one of the most important features of genuine manliness.
>
> —Stephen Mansfield

Strength is the glory of manhood and fatherhood. Many a man has failed in life for no other reason save he was weak. He had a good heart, but he was weak. He was popular, generous, gentlemanly, but weak. Men and fathers who quit when things get tough not only set that example of how a man acts for his sons and daughters, they also leave them in precarious situations. The physical, emotional, psychological, and financial challenges of children from father-absent homes are well-documented. Guys, nothing harms your children as much as them observing you not practicing what you preach. If they observe you quitting, lying, cheating, or being unfaithful, it will devastate their character.

Author Dennis Rainey talks about the need for men and fathers to "step up." Here's how he describes what happens when they don't:

> What's the opposite of stepping up? Standing still . . . lying down . . . becoming a couch potato. Male passivity is a disease that robs a man of his purpose while it destroys marriages, ruins families, and spoils legacies. A passive man doesn't engage; he retreats. He neglects personal responsibility. At its core, passivity is cowardice.[2]

I can't think of any phase of fathering that I have been through that has been easy. Frankly, the older my kids get, the harder it becomes. It's difficult being a father and raising a family. It's difficult leading a family, especially today. But your family relies upon your strength. They cannot thrive without your presence and masculine essence. Your protection and provision keep them safe from harm, and your presence keeps them bonded and secure.

Part of having strength (both internal and external) is to exercise it. Men need to lead physically aggressive lives. As author Stephen Mansfield says, "They need contest and conquest, strain and struggle. Otherwise, we lose ourselves to softness and effeminacy."[3]

My brother-in-law recently asked me why I trained so hard and put myself through the abuse of running in another one of the popular cross-country obstacle/mud races that are sweeping the nation. I didn't have an answer for him at the time—it was just a way to challenge myself. But I now realize that as a man I was feeling a natural desire to push myself to my limits in competition with others. I was feeling soft and untested. I needed an aggressive conquest in my life—something I achieved by the strain of my sinew and the grit of my determination. When I finished, I don't know that I felt any manlier, but I sure felt good about having completed it. I felt satisfied with my masculinity.

But pushing myself physically also helps to develop intestinal fortitude, perseverance, and a host of other character traits within me. I need those traits to continue on—to stay and not leave—when the stresses of providing for a family become too much, when my marriage is struggling, or when my life is beating me down.

I do it because I want to be a better dad.

9

Children, Members of the Family

Not the Center of the Universe

Fathers are to sons what blacksmiths are to swords. It is the job of the blacksmith not only to make the sword but also to maintain its edge of sharpness. It is the job of the father to keep his son sharp and save him from dullness of foolishness. He gives his son that sharp edge through discipline.

—Steve Farrar, *King Me: What Every Son Wants and Needs from His Father*

Your children are gifts from God and should be celebrated as welcome members of the family. But they are not the *center* of the family. Your marriage is the center—the cornerstone—of the family.

A lot of parental dissatisfaction is rooted in unrealistic expectations. When we have unrealistic or idealistic expectations of what it is like to be a father or how our children will turn out, we are setting ourselves up for disappointment. Understand that you can be a good parent and it doesn't necessarily mean your children will turn out well. Just like you can be a bad parent and it doesn't mean your children will automatically turn out to be bad people. Certainly having good parents gives children an advantage in life, and bad parents often pass negative programming on to their children, but your children have free will, and so just like you they can choose to be the kind of individuals they want and the behaviors they want to engage in. We've all seen kids from good homes make bad choices and end up involved in drugs or crime. We've also seen people from horrendous homes who turned out to be outstanding citizens and live very healthy, happy, and successful lives.

Developing Healthy Self-Esteem but Not Entitlement

Children today are overwhelmed by the choices they have. Whether it is channels on TV or types of shoes, there are simply too many options for virtually anything they want. It overloads the ability of most children to function and make good choices. Parents need to allow their children to have choices, but allowing a five-year-old to have an equal vote in all scenarios of life and family seems a bit much. Our friend's neighbor allowed her ten-year-old daughter to choose her school path (through college) with no paternal input because the girl thought the alternative school she visited looked "fun." Parents today are giving children endless choices and the decision-making privileges that simply do not correspond to their abilities. This is helping to create (among other things) an incredibly "entitled" generation.

Children need firm but loving discipline and guidelines. Fathers need to remain confident in their positions of authority, as kids will have a tendency to try to exploit Mom's weaknesses. Let me explain that before I start getting nasty letters. Mothers typically love their children unconditionally as opposed to a more performance-based love from fathers. Children need both of those types of loving and disciplinary styles to grow up healthy and whole. Together those natural tendencies likely reflect the differing aspects of God's loving character. Moms are also innately more nurturing and loving. Hence they often will allow children to do things that in the long run may not be good for them—like giving in too easily. Children interpret that as a weakness and try to exploit it whenever possible. Obviously, not all moms are like that, and frankly my wife was a lot more likely to say "No!" to more things than I was with our children. But when children can play on a mom's emotions to their advantage, they will. (Kids tend to be little psychological Machiavellians.) Dad has to be united with her to help enforce rules and boundaries. The same goes with you, Dad. If you are an old softy and Mom is the stricter disciplinarian in the house, you need to acknowledge the value she brings in balancing out the family. If you think kids can't manipulate Dad as well, just wait until you have a teenage daughter—you'll be like putty in her hands. It's the first thing they learn to do—they practice on Dad so they learn the ins and outs of dealing effectively with the male gender.

Self-Worth Should Not Be a Burden to Others

As important as our children are, they are not all-important. Children who hold a place of utmost importance in the family are a burden to their parents and anyone else they happen to come in contact with. I can't tell you how many times a bratty grade-schooler has ruined our evening out in a restaurant because her parents feverishly rushed around trying to meet all her outrageous demands, expecting everyone around them to submit to her princess-like charms. Or the parents who allow their children to run amok in the grocery store like wild savages. These parents seem to place no expectations upon their children beyond what they themselves can do *for* them. A better way is to have realistic expectations that stretch your child without breaking him (or the people around him).

To develop a healthy self-esteem in our children, we must have high expectations for them, but not too high. When we expect or demand a child (who has never been an adult) to think, act, or do things as an adult, we produce impotence, frustration, and even hostility in our children (like the child running wild in the market). It destroys a child's belief in their own capabilities. Have you ever asked your children, "What were you thinking?" or "Why can't you ever . . . ?" or "How many times do I have to tell you?" We have the expectation that they understand something we, as an adult, take for granted. Likely they were thinking like a child and that was why they did not understand what was expected of them.

I often had unrealistic or unfair expectations of my kids while they were growing up. Not so much behaviorally as intellectually. I expected that they would understand concepts that were above their level of development. You can't expect a two-year-old to remember all the house rules and obey them all the time. Their minds are not capable of processing or recalling that kind of information. And even though teenagers might act like two-year-olds a lot of the time, they can in fact process and recall house rules all the time should they so choose.

Our children also have to feel valued in order to develop healthy self-esteem. The only way a parent can make a child feel valued is if the child trusts them. Trust between people is established by three conditions: knowing that the other person is listening, knowing that we can risk our feelings without having them discounted, and knowing that the person believes what we have to offer is significant. Without those, we cannot trust others or believe what they say.

Is Self-Value Earned or Bestowed?

For all intents and purposes, our children (and maybe us as well) are the first generation of children who were not raised in a family network where they contributed to the family's well-being. Before 1930 the majority of people in this country lived on farms. Within twenty to thirty years the majority moved to cities, causing a huge shift in family dynamics. In rural homes and farms, all the children contributed to the family—through daily chores, work, and even earning income—and so they were important and they made a difference in the family's well-being. Without that sense of importance, our children grow up feeling insignificant and without value. Many kids today in urban/suburban homes are virtually ignored (if not resented) as parents go about the daily task of working and providing for the family—evidenced by the latchkey kid syndrome. They seldom contribute anything of value to the family beyond their presence.[1] While many kids today are the focal point of the family agenda (being shuttled to and fro for a multitude of activities), they still do not contribute anything meaningful to the family besides the "gloriousness" of their presence.

Being ignored causes the same chemical reactions in the brain as experiencing a physical injury. The only difference is that physical pain goes away, but the pain of lost love doesn't.[2] Make no mistake, our kids know that we spend our time on things that are important to us. The average American parent spends very little time each day in direct communication with their children. Since kids evaluate how loved they are by the amount of time we spend with them, what kind of message are we sending our children?

Kids who do not feel valued or that their lives have significance are more likely to commit suicide, compulsively engage in sex with people they don't know (or sometimes don't even like), or receive impressions about their worth from the media. Kids raised in a TV "reality" fail to learn valuable life skills such as patience, personal initiative, hard work, and delayed gratification.[3]

A father's and mother's eyes are the first and most important mirror that children have to learn about themselves. If that mirror reflects back that the child is capable, important, significant, and loved, then the child will believe that about themselves. That perception is important because we know that children who believe they are capable of doing something will do something. Those who believe they can't, won't.

Educator and speaker Richard Lavoie uses the analogy of poker chips when talking about a child's self-esteem. Each time a child does something well or achieves something, we give them a compliment, which is similar to giving them a poker chip (or a bundle of chips if it's really good). When something bad happens to kids, it takes away poker chips. Our goal as parents is to make sure our kids have more poker chips when they go to bed each night than they did when they awoke that morning. Kids from healthy families eventually build up a big pile of poker chips. Unfortunately kids from unhealthy homes tend to get few or no poker chips each day. Hence they tend to not have any poker chips to spare—they hold on tight to the few they have. So when it comes time to answer a question in class, stand up for a bullied classmate, or try something new, a child is risking their poker chips by potentially failing. Because they have a lot of chips, kids with good self-esteem are willing to risk their chips because they have plenty to spare. Kids with low self-esteem aren't willing because they don't have enough to risk losing any.[4]

Dads, because your words and actions are so powerful, you have the ability to either take away a lot of chips from your children or give them a ton of chips to deal with in life. Make sure your child has a lot of chips at the end of each day.

Respect—Earned or Given?

Your children may be the only people you will meet in the entire world who want to love and respect you. They have an internal need to love and respect their father. They may be the only people from whom you do not have to initially earn their respect—they automatically respect you because they *want* to respect you. Now, *we* can do things to cause them to lose that desire to respect us, but it is still present inside all human beings. Growing up in an alcoholic home, I craved a father I could love and respect. And I will tell you that when I met my biological father for the first time at age twenty-four, I knew he was a man I could love and respect. As our relationship has developed over the years, a lot of healing has occurred inside me just by having a father who I can look up to, but also one who loves and respects me in return.

So if it is true that our children instinctively respect their fathers, shouldn't we cultivate that gift by being the kind of men they can respect? Also, in order to *get* respect, we often have to *give* respect first. Through behaviors that show a lack of respect to our children (threatening, correcting, or directing them too much), we run the risk of squelching their enthusiasm for learning, growing, and gathering information on their own for fear of disappointing us.

It seems disrespectful to be overly directive of our children. By always jumping in and telling them what to do, how to do it, and when it should be done, we are basically telling them they are not smart enough to figure simple things out on their own. I understand how tempting it is to do that when we have little time and lots to do. But as often as possible, try to allow your children to think through the process of solving a problem or completing a task on their own. We all learn in incremental stages; we scaffold knowledge upon what we have previously learned—not all at once. So children will likely be marginally successful at new tasks, making some mistakes but getting a little bit better each time they attempt them. Children cannot gain wisdom as long as they are afraid to try something or as long as we analyze it for them.

One of my biggest downfalls as a father was being impatient with my children's failures and having the expectation that just because I knew something, they should as well. Do my kids respect me a little less for that? Maybe. But maybe they respect themselves just a little less because of it as well. Maybe the inability to live up to Dad's expectations caused them to shut down a part of themselves rather than try and then get criticized for their efforts. It hurts me to admit that, but I'd rather see you learn from my experience than carry around the same regrets that I do for it.

Raising Kids You Like

We all love our children, but do we actually like them? Are your children likable human beings that you (and others) enjoy spending time with? Here's what one parent said about how children are raised today:

> One of the things I've learned since I quit working to stay home is that the more I'm with them, the less tolerant I am of their bad behavior. When you spend long stretches of time with your children, you begin to require of them that they be decent people who are pleasurable to be around. Most of us can tolerate bratty spoiled kids for about an hour. It's hard to be around them for much longer than that. I think that as a society we are raising a generation of kids who are lazy, sarcastic, and demanding and have a tremendous sense of entitlement. And it's our fault. We have the best intentions. We want them to have the best of everything, we're worried about their self-esteem. But in an effort to give them what we never had, we seem to have lost the courage to say no. I've been as guilty as the next guy and I want to recognize my errant ways and make the necessary changes while there's still time.[5]

Most of us enter parenthood believing that our children are a blank slate just waiting for us to shower our wisdom upon them. Unfortunately, most children seem to be resistant of our teaching—usually for their entire lives! Not only that, they seem determined to mimic our faults while resisting our values, expectations, and dreams.[6]

Our children tend to bring out the best and worst in us. They grow us as human beings. Parenting brings out all our faults and anxieties, while teaching us how to love unconditionally.

Here are some tips to keep in mind to raise likable children:

- Don't over-parent (be a helicopter parent).
- Don't under-parent (be overly permissive).
- Don't be too authoritarian. Good parents set firm, loving boundaries without showing anger, lecturing, or using threats.
- Do have high expectations for them.
- Do treat them with respect.
- Do teach them manners and hold them accountable.

Your children will fare much better in life if they are likable than if they are insufferable little snots. Do them (and yourself) a favor and teach them the basic tenets of being civilized human beings.

Children Are Natural-Born Liars

A friend of mine thinks all kids are natural-born liars. He may be right. I've yet to see a kid who won't lie at the drop of a hat to stay out of trouble. When you walk into a room and see him with chocolate all over his mug and ask him, "Did you eat all the chocolate cake?" he will always say, "No." You know he ate it because he's got chocolate all over himself, the cake tray is empty, and there are cake crumbs all over the floor at his feet. He's caught red-handed (or brown-handed in this case). Yet, he will still instinctively lie in order to try to avoid getting in trouble—it's human nature to do it. Even Adam and Eve did it. In circumstances like these—when you know the answer to a question—don't ask. That way he won't be forced to lie to you. Maybe just ask him why he ate the cake. If you put him into situations where he is forced to lie enough, he'll eventually get used to it.

Children are more intelligent than we generally give them credit for, and they are surprisingly adept at psychological warfare. For example, have you ever told your child to do a chore only to have them either not do it ("I forgot") or give a 500-reason treatise why they can't do it right now? Often a parent will get frustrated and order the child to do it "this instant!" Faced now with no choice (but not wanting to be forced to do something they don't like), they capitulate but make you wish they hadn't. They might "accidently" break one of your favorite plates while washing the dishes (all very apologetically, of course), or move at a snail's pace while doing the chore, which keeps the family from attending a scheduled event. Or the child might even lie and say they did the chore when they really haven't, knowing they won't suffer the consequences until they have gotten whatever reward they desire more (going to the movies, out for ice cream, etc.). This frustrates the parent to no end, generally making it easier to do the chore ourselves rather than put up with such shenanigans.

A better strategy (and one that generally prevents lying) is to give your child choices. Instead of ordering them to eat their dinner, say something like, "You're welcome to eat what is for dinner, or you can wait and see if the next meal appeals to you more." Instead of demanding they clean their room, tell them, "Feel free to join us for dinner as soon as your room is cleaned." Or for chores maybe, "Would you rather take out the trash first or clean your room?" This gives children a sense of control, and since you are not making the choice for them, they don't feel that sense of rebelliousness. This works equally well with toddlers and teens. Just make sure that all the choices you give them are ones you want to happen. It's difficult to lie about something when you make the decision.

Lying becomes very prevalent at the onset of puberty when kids, already overwhelmed with changing bodies and roller-coaster emotions, just want parents and others to think well of them. Younger children can lie as a form of asserting their independence but still want the love of their parents. The most common form of lying is when a child answers a parent's question with "I don't know." Usually the child does know but recognizes that the parent doesn't really want an answer to their question. Ever asked these questions of your child? "Why do you always . . .?" or "Why can't you ever . . .?" or even "How many times do I have to tell you . . .?" Those are rhetorical questions that parents ask to which they don't really want an answer. They are either making a point or are trying to humiliate and shame the child.[7]

One last thing to remember: when our kids do something wrong (like whack their sibling upside the head) and we force them to say "I'm sorry" (especially if they are not), we are really only teaching them to lie. We always have to make them say it again "like you mean it." While it is important that they develop empathy and compassion, a better way might be to make them take some quiet time and come up with their own solution to the issue. You will probably still have to "help" them apologize, but at least they'll be more sincere about it.

Better dads know that.

Disciplining Your Children

> The value of marriage is not that adults produce children but that children produce adults.
>
> —Peter De Vries

Like a lot of people of my age group, I was raised in a home that used a good amount of corporal punishment to program us to not do things we weren't supposed to do. The problem with physical punishment is that by its very nature it is performed most often when the parent is angry—which is never a good time to teach a lesson. Corporal punishment not only hurts the child but it hurts the parent and their relationship as well. I've come to recognize that discipline and not punishment is a better way to parent our children.

I'll also admit that I've changed my attitude on this subject over the years. As a younger father I believed that since my parents used it and I turned out okay, then it must be okay for my kids. Not that our kids were subject to many spankings (at least not as many as they think they were), but I wasn't in the camp of the "any spanking is child abuse" proponents. Here's why I changed my opinion on this controversial subject.

The goal of discipline is to teach, not to punish. While punishment is often done in anger, we seldom discipline in anger. Punishment is something you do *to* a child, discipline is what you do *for* a child. Discipline uses logic and a considered plan to teach a lesson. Punishment's nature is to inflict pain in order to make a little person want to avoid that consequence of the behavior in the future. That's not to say that a swat on the butt when a small child is doing something life-threateningly dangerous won't be remembered and avoided—just like if you mouth off to a bully and get popped in the nose, you're likely to not try that again real soon. But in general a better way to discipline kids is to use it as a teaching lesson and not an opportunity to inflict pain.

I recently watched a video on Facebook of a Middle Eastern man beating his adult male slave with a belt. It was brutal to watch and made me somewhat sick to my stomach. But it was not all that much different from what I remember from my experiences as a child being spanked with a belt. Perhaps if each of us were forced to watch ourselves spanking our children, we would find other ways to discipline them.

We often hear the adage "Spare the rod, spoil the child" used when referring to disciplining children. That's generally taken to mean if you don't use the rod on them, they will end up being spoiled brats. And kids who are not subject to healthy discipline do tend to become insufferable little monsters. But when that passage was written, a "rod" was used as a tool by shepherds for *guiding* their sheep, not inflicting pain upon them.[8]

Additionally, the portion of the brain (pre-frontal cortex) that controls decision making and impulse control doesn't

Differences between Discipline vs. Punishment

While discipline and punishment might have similar goals (managing and improving a child's behavior), they are vastly different in their approach and the impression they leave on a child.

Discipline	Punishment
Used before, during & after an event	Used only after an event
Teaches	Enforces
Based on the child's development & ability to change	Denies child's ability to change
Respects child	Disrespects child
Educates child	Inflicts pain on child
Teaches internal self-control	Managed by exter-nal control
Builds trust	Builds resentment
Anger to remorse	Anger to revenge
Increases child's self-esteem	Decreases child's self-esteem
Parent feels satisfaction	Parent feels guilty

fully develop in human beings until the child is in their late twenties. Therefore, punishment may be counterproductive in that they may sometimes make bad decisions even if they don't intend to. But by using positive discipline techniques, your children will automatically learn from them regardless of their level of brain development. Positive rewards are a much more powerful learning and motivating device than are negative or hurtful consequences. While fear of punishment may be a motivating emotion, it only works until the child gets bigger than the parent. Healthy discipline teaches lessons that last a lifetime.

Using Discipline

But that doesn't mean that children do not need guidelines, limits, and boundaries. In fact, they need limits—they're essential to healthy maturity. A 1967 study by Stanley Coopersmith showed that the parents who gave their kids the most rules and limitations had children with the highest self-esteem, while those who gave their children the most freedoms had kids with the lowest self-esteem.[9] The difference between boundaries and "non-negotiables" mentioned earlier is that boundaries give children choices, non-negotiables don't. So how do we use discipline (as opposed to punishment) to help set healthy limits for our children?

First, understand that if you use discipline consistently when your children are young (toddlers), it makes disciplining them later much easier. Be sure they clearly understand the rules of your home. At this stage you have to provide a lot of guidance, training them all the time. Teaching children to listen to and obey you when they are little allows you to relax the rules as they get older. But this takes a lot of work when they are young.

All forms of discipline have common components that should be followed:

1. Be consistent and fair. Consistency is important in establishing trust and helping your children understand your expectations. If you change the rules all the time, you can't expect them to know what they are.

2. Use appropriate consequences for each offense.
3. Present a united front with your spouse.
4. Give more praise than correction. Avoid long lectures.
5. Tailor discipline to fit your child's bent.
6. Know the developmental phases that your children go through at different ages.

When you are contemplating disciplining a child's behavior, take into consideration a few factors to determine how severe the discipline should be:

- Is this behavior typical or part of normal childhood development? A two-year-old (or a teenager) is going to act like a two-year-old from time to time no matter how good the child normally behaves.
- Does the behavior occur at any specific time or occasion? If a child only starts misbehaving or has a bad attitude right before dinner, perhaps there are issues like blood sugar levels or other factors involved.
- Consider questions like *Why would a child act this way? Is this typical behavior of other children or specific to your child? Is the behavior dangerous, destructive, or illegal* (certainly any of these three would warrant a stronger response than a minor infraction of family rules)? *What are the long-range consequences of this behavior?* Considering those things might give you an idea on how important it is to intervene.
- Last, stay calm and pick your battles. Not everything is worthy of an all-out war. If you fight all the battles, you will eventually lose the war.

One strategy that works well in modifying children's behavior is to allow them to participate in designing their consequences. That sounds counterintuitive but works surprisingly well. While setting up or discussing a family value, get your child's input on what the consequences should be if he misbehaves. If you haven't already developed a consequence, you can ask your children what they think is a fair and reasonable idea. That's not to say you don't determine the consequence as a parent, but this at least helps children take ownership of and buy into the program. Without that buy-in children feel like they have no control over their circumstances, and all of us want control over our lives.

Healthy discipline should also have several goals in mind. The first is to build trust between the parent and the child. Trust is the foundation of all healthy human relationships. Lack of trust in a person inhibits their ability to develop a conscience. Once you discipline your child, don't hold a grudge. The slate is wiped clean and you are starting over—sort of like how God forgives us when we sin and ask for forgiveness. He doesn't hold it against us but forgets all about it.

The second goal is to build self-esteem in the child. If we punish kids too often, they begin to believe themselves unworthy and *unable* to be good. As dads we need to change the belief behind the behavior, not just the behavior. If our children believe they are not capable of being a good person, it doesn't matter how much we discipline them; they still will not be able to change that perception—any change will only be temporary. Our kids' perception of themselves is the key to their attitude, motivation, and behavior. If they believe themselves capable of something, they will be. If they believe they can't do something, they won't even try. Even though

The Three R's of Punishment[10]

1. *Resentment*: "This is unfair. I can't trust adults."
2. *Revenge*: "They are winning now, but I'll get even."
3. *Retreat, in one of three extremes*:
   a. *Rebellion*: "I'll do what I want and just be more careful not to get caught next time. I have a right to lie and cheat under these circumstances."
   b. *Reduced self-esteem*: "I must really be a bad person who deserves to be punished. I will keep trying to please, but I'm not much good at it."
   c. *Retirement*: "I give up. I can't win, so why try? I wish people would just leave me alone."

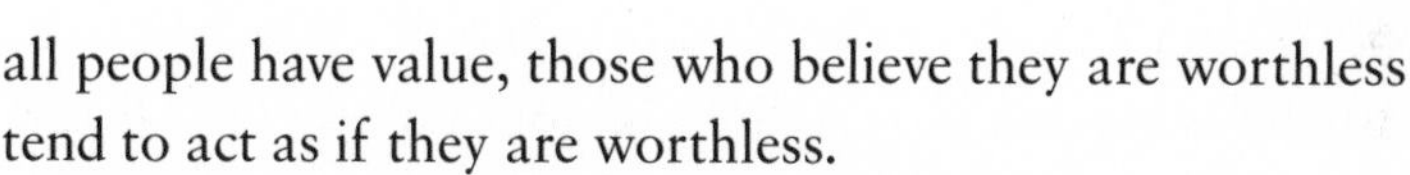

all people have value, those who believe they are worthless tend to act as if they are worthless.

Next is to teach new behaviors. We don't know what we don't know. A child who has never been exposed to a situation or doesn't know (or is too young to know) the rules of a new circumstance cannot be expected to know how to act or what the boundaries are. Part of a parent's job is to teach our children how to live life successfully. The best time to learn things is when we make mistakes. It's also important to understand that we learn in stages—knowledge is accumulative. We build on understanding something by what we've previously learned. So often we have to repeat mistakes in order to learn the entire lesson.

Discipline also allows parents to re-teach exisiting negative behaviors. That's why it's never too late to change the way you relate to your children. Even teenagers with established bad habits or behaviors can be "reprogrammed" through consistent discipline.

Last, discipline (as opposed to punishment in which they have no control) helps a child gain self-control. It teaches them how to think for themselves and how to act in the future when faced with similar situations. They must learn how to manage and control themselves. We can't be with our kids twenty-four hours a day, but we want them to hear our voice whispering in their ear when faced with circumstances that could be troublesome or potentially dangerous for them.

Also remember that consequences should be used for both negative *and* positive situations (good consequences for positive situations and bad consequences for negative situations). Remember to reward the behaviors you like just as you discipline the ones you want to correct.

Always remember to follow through with whatever consequences you set for violations of your family rules. If you don't follow through (every single time), everything you do or say will be ignored. We've all seen the parent who keeps repeating "This is the last time!" or that continues to count to three over and over again. These parents have children who are in control of the relationship.

If you do follow through with consequences, it usually only takes a couple of times for children to stop testing the limits of their boundaries. This works no matter how old they are—again, it's never too late to change behaviors (in us or them). Mostly we want to remember that discipline while parenting requires us to use firmness, dignity, and respect when exercising our authority.

You can't force your children to obey you. Well, maybe you can—for a while anyway. But eventually they will rebel and disobey you if for no other reason than they can. Also, children can be compliant on the outside and still be disobedient on the inside. That's one reason why screaming, yelling, threatening, and repeating yourself are such ineffective strategies.

When your children become eighteen years old, you probably won't be around all the time to yell at them and force them to make the right decision. A big-picture vision of raising children is to tell them what you expect from them, what the benefits are if they obey, and what the consequences are if they don't. Then let them choose. Of course, that requires you to be very diligent in making sure you follow through with said consequences (both positive and negative). But the goal is to teach them how to make decisions and to know that each decision has consequences. That's a much better way to approach life successfully—especially when they move out of the house and out from under your protection and guidance.

Finally, some of you may have children who are more challenging than others. They may not be able to learn things easily, may struggle in school, and may generally seem unruly or hyperactive and unable to focus. Before allowing the school (or anyone else) to label them as having Attention Deficit Disorder (ADD) or Attention Deficit Hyperactivity Disorder (ADHD), you should consider a few things. First, all children develop at differing rates and schedules (boys are usually a few years behind girls until adolescence). Additionally, the education format used in public schools is generally not conducive to the way most boys learn best. Boys typically struggle with sitting quietly for long periods of time while being lectured to (I still do and to my knowledge I don't have ADD). Recesses and PE are being cut back, which especially harms boys, who need that release of pent-up energy.

Diagnosing ADHD with any degree of certainty is difficult—primarily because the symptoms (distractibility, impulsivity, and hyperactivity) are consistent with normal behavior in all young children. The challenge is really this: Is the child exhibiting *more* of any of those traits than he should be for his age? Since nearly all preschoolers exhibit these symptoms, a child shouldn't be diagnosed before the age of seven or older. Additionally, ADHD-like symptoms such as distractibility or hyperactivity can also be caused by a variety of other conditions, including sleep disorders, anxiety, or even cultural differences.[11]

To better avoid misdiagnosis, we need to be aware of the distinction between ADD and a child being distractible. Kids with ADD pay attention to nothing. Kids who are distractible pay attention to everything.

Also if your child has been traumatized (which could be anything from having been through a family divorce to having been physically injured in some way), he or she may suffer from some form of Post-Traumatic Stress Disorder (PTSD). PTSD and ADHD have very similar symptoms in educational environments, especially in boys. Yet they are very different issues—one is a physical reaction to a traumatic event and the other is a chemical imbalance. Unfortunately, many children with PTSD are misdiagnosed with ADHD and given a stimulant such as Ritalin, which only exacerbates the problem. PTSD is an anxiety disorder (not a concentration issue) and is treated with anti-anxiety medication, pretty much the exact opposite of a stimulant. You can see how that might cause problems.

I am not saying ADD and ADHD are not legitimate diagnoses in some children, but I think too many children today (especially boys) are medicated for just being boys or for being naturally rambunctious.

A better dad makes sure his children are protected from unnecessary and inaccurate labeling, medical procedures, and medication.

10

Not in My House

Dad, the Gatekeeper of the Home

> How can anyone enter a strong man's house and carry off his possessions unless he first ties up the strong man? Then he can plunder his house.
>
> —Matthew 12:29

The verse above speaks directly to fathers. Virtually everything our culture promotes involves plundering our home and carrying off our children. Thankfully, one person has the power to offset the world's teaching and influence on their children. That person is Dad.

Whether or not we want the responsibility, as fathers, we *are* the gatekeeper of our home. Mothers might be the decision makers in the home, but without Dad alongside her to reinforce (and enforce) her decisions, rules might not be as well

How Jim Bowie's Toughness Made the Bowie Knife Famous

On September 19, 1827, Jim Bowie and Major Norris Wright attended a duel on a sandbar outside of Natchez, Mississippi. The duelists were Samuel Levi Wells III (whom Bowie supported) and Dr. Thomas Harris Maddox (whom Wright favored). Each side also brought a number of supporters.

The duel began with each man firing two shots, and, since neither man was injured, they resolved their duel with a handshake. As the duelists turned to leave, Bowie stepped toward them. Apparently, interpreting this as an aggressive move, Maddox's friends ran forward toward the group.

Seeing an opportunity for revenge, one of the men fired at a man he had previously dueled against. Unfortunately, he missed and struck Bowie in the hip, knocking him to the ground. The two bystanders fired at each other, one being wounded, with the original antagonist being killed.

Bowie, rising to his feet, drew his knife and charged at the survivor, who struck him so hard with his empty pistol upon the head that it broke and knocked Bowie to his knees. Another man appeared, drew a pistol, and shot at the fallen Bowie, but missed. He then drew his sword cane and stabbed Bowie in

established and followed. Fathers have an innate authority with children—maybe even a fear factor. Perhaps it's because fathers are larger, stronger, have shorter tempers, and are louder with deeper voices. Dads can be downright scary to kids sometimes. That power, used to an extreme, is detrimental. But used effectively and responsibly, it serves a good purpose.

The Bible is clear about Dad's importance in this area when it states, "In fact, no one can enter a strong man's house without first tying him up. Then he can plunder the strong man's house" (Mark 3:27).

the chest, but the thin blade was deflected by his sternum. As the attacker attempted to pull the blade free, Bowie reached up, grabbed the man's shirt, and pulled him down upon the point of his knife, killing him instantly. Bowie, with a sword still protruding from his chest, was shot again and stabbed by another member of the group. As Bowie stood, pulling the sword cane from his chest, two brothers then fired at him, striking him in the arm. Bowie spun and cut off part of the brother's forearm. The second brother fired a second shot at Bowie, but missed, causing both to flee.

The Battle of the Sandbar lasted more than 10 minutes, leaving two men dead and another four men wounded. The doctors who had been present for the duel managed to patch Bowie's wounds. One doctor reportedly said, "How he [Bowie] lived is a mystery to me, but live he did."

Newspapers picked up the story, which became famous nationally. Bowie's fighting prowess and his knife were described in detail. Eyewitnesses agreed that Bowie did not attack first, and the others had focused their attack on Bowie because "they considered him the most dangerous man among their opposition." After the Sandbar Fight and subsequent battles in which Bowie successfully used his knife to defend himself, his knife became very popular.[1]

Dads need to be tough in order to guard their homes and keep their families safe. Our kids look up to us to provide for and protect them. I was at the doctor's office today. A little girl (under two?) was there getting a shot. As she received the injection, she started crying, "Daddy, Daddy!" Afterward she wanted Mommy to console and nurture her, but her initial instinct was to cry for Daddy to protect her from harm and pain.

Dads not only need to be physically tough but emotionally tough too. That's because Dad provides not only physical protection but also guards against unhealthy mental and emotional attacks as well. A dad who walks with the Lord also provides spiritual protection for his family.

Years ago I had a friend who, as I look back, was a pretty tough guy. Once we went wilderness camping with our young sons in the Eagle Creek area of the Columbia River Gorge between the states of Oregon and Washington. After hiking up the mountainside about seven miles, we decided to camp for the night. About 100 yards off the trail was a beautiful pond and waterfall, where we went to wash off and cool down. Somehow in the pool he slipped on some rocks and hurt his ankle. I didn't think much about it because he barely mentioned it. The next day we hiked back down the mountain and went home. We soon found out he had actually broken his ankle. I thought that was pretty tough—hiking down a mountainside seven miles on a broken ankle with a three-year-old on his shoulders. That is until a little while later he went horseback riding with his little girl. He didn't know much about horseback riding but was determined to impress his daughter. Well, the horse apparently bucked when he wasn't expecting it and he popped straight up in the air and came down on the saddle wrong. He ended up with testicles the size of cantaloupes for the next two weeks. Interestingly, he only missed two days of work. I don't know if his little girl was impressed or not, but I sure was.

But being physically tough and domestically tough are two different things. Many dads are physically tough guys who do not hesitate to fight for their kids but back off and don't protect their children from the culture rushing in to grab them. When Dad is passive, apathetic, embarrassed to intervene, or even just nonchalant about the cultural influences entering his home, he is allowing himself to be "tied up" so that his home can be plundered.

Let's look at some of the areas where a father needs to control the environment of his home by controlling what comes in the front door.

Why It's Important to Help Choose Your Child's Friends

Many parents are uncomfortable with interfering with the friends their children choose. But friends can do great damage. Many a parent has seen twenty years of hard work flushed down the toilet by their child spending twenty minutes around the wrong person. You wouldn't consider allowing a child to have access to a medicine cabinet full of poisonous drugs. So why would you allow them unlimited access to friends who could be just as dangerous to their health as any chemical? You also wouldn't allow your older children to hang around with pimps or drug pushers, but some of the young people they go to school with are apprenticing for those jobs even now.

There's an old adage that "opposites attract." Young people (especially those from safe, healthy homes) are often attracted to kids with a dangerous or rebellious bent to them. Our daughter, because of a compassionate heart, always felt compelled to try to help at-risk girls from single-parent homes. Later, in her teens, she liked to associate with the "bad kids" because it gave her rebellious spirit a thrill as she revolted against (in her mind) her "too safe and boring" home life. If you are interested in the chronicles of those adventurous times, check out my book *Becoming the Dad Your Daughter Needs*. For the sake of keeping the rest of my hair, I'll not repeat any of them here. But understand that regardless of how good a parent you and your wife are, even the best of kids can be lured into making bad decisions and end up in dangerous situations by the friends they choose. That's why better dads actively participate in knowing their children's friends.

Show Me Your Friends and I'll Show You Your Future

My brother-in-law told me once that you are the sum total of your five closest friends. Your friends and the people you hang around with most will influence you even if you don't think they will. As 1 Corinthians 15:33 says, "Bad company corrupts good character." Always. As a dad you have an obligation to know your children's friends *and* their parents—even when your kids are teenagers (maybe especially when they are teens).

We were lucky that for most of the way through high school our daughter was friends with girls she played sports with and our son was friends with guys he either went to church with or was in Boy Scouts with. Hence, we knew most of their friends' parents pretty well. However, when our daughter went through a rough patch during her later years in high school, she quit sports and started hanging around with kids who were obviously bad influences on her. Even in those circumstances we tried to meet their parents (that was fun) and always tried to invite these young people into our home as much as possible (that was even more fun). There were still young people we did not want her hanging around with and we had to convince her why they were not wise choices in friends—not so much by forbidding her to see them as by calmly and rationally using examples that she could not defend them against. We could usually accurately predict the choices these young people would make in certain situations and then predict the outcome and consequences of their decisions. It allowed our daughter to see that we didn't have anything against her friends; we just wanted the best for her. Rather than harangue her with a lecture or criticize her friends (which was tempting), we found that if we treated her with respect, then she in turn respected us. That respect caused her to follow our wishes even when she would have rather not. That respect also allowed us to have influence in her life even when we were distant in our relationship.

Better dads make it a point to know their children's friends and the parents of those friends.

Too Much Media

> Their children are overweight, unlettered, and for the most part untested. They watch movies on iPods and read almost not at all. Worse still, from an old man's point of view, is that they have been taught that love must be offered without judgment, and thus grow up strangers to a sense of shame.
>
> —Thomas H. Cook, *Master of the Delta*

Our society and the families that comprise it are changing rapidly. We have evolved from a rural culture to an urban/ suburban society over the past fifty years. In smaller, rural settings children within families were offered the opportunity to learn life skills through on-the-job training and were needed to help the family survive. Today's children are no longer needed in the day-to-day functions of the family and many fail to learn the skills needed to become capable adults. Instead, they spend large quantities of time watching television, playing video games, or interfacing with "friends" on social media. Today, most parents work outside the home (many with long hours) and don't spend as much time with children as generations past—instead they give them things to compensate for their absence. This makes it difficult to raise capable, self-reliant children who are prepared to be successful adults. In their book, *Raising Self-Reliant Children in a Self-Indulgent World*, authors H. Stephen Glenn and Jane Nelsen say this about children: "Without a meaningful role in the family, it is difficult to develop a sense of meaning, purpose, and significance through being needed, listened to, and taken seriously."[2]

The latest brain research shows that the brains of young children who watch too much TV do not develop properly.[3] Too much TV can be a very real detriment to children on many levels. I understand how tempting it can be to use the TV as a distraction (or a babysitter) so that you can get something done or have some much-needed time to yourself. Especially as kids get older, most families do not have a plan for the amount of TV their children watch. Many of us just have the TV on as background noise. We watch whatever is on. Have you ever channel surfed over and over, trying to find something good to watch? When you can't, you end up watching the best of the worst.

Since most kids watch multiple hours of TV a day, a good plan might be to limit television time to, say, one to three hours a day (or less). The American Academy of Pediatrics recently updated its recommendations regarding children and TV. They recommend for children under two to watch no television, and for older children no more than two hours per day.[4]

Don't let your children have a TV in their room. Instead, find other things to fill that time, such as interactive board games like Monopoly or outside games like kick the can or hide-and-seek. Those old-fashioned activities require physical social interaction, which is lacking from the average child's life today. Kids also need more physical activity. Our children are becoming increasingly obese. Find activities to keep them active and outdoors in the fresh air. For some reason the moms in our neighborhood don't allow their children to play out in the rain. We live in Oregon, so that means that their children are indoors about eight to nine months a year. Someone (Dad) needs to tell those moms that rain, dirt, and mud are all good for children.

Kids today (boys especially) spend too many hours a week playing computer video games. Research shows that kids between the ages of 8 and 18 spend an average of 44.5 hours a week in front of their computer screen. Nearly one-third of boys and about 23 percent of all kids today feel like they are "addicted to video games."[5] Video games in particular provide visual and hand-eye coordination competition, which is very attractive to the brains of young males. Unfortunately, they are probably also responsible for overstimulating their minds, causing them to be uninterested in reality and relationships, which seem boring by comparison. Combine that with the significant challenges that pornography produces in males of all ages, and many young men today are unable to have healthy relationships with females; are checking out of life, causing them to be undereducated and either unemployed or underemployed; and are generally "failing to launch" into life.

Surveys indicate that up to 93 percent of boys and 62 percent of girls have viewed pornography before they turn 18 years of age. At least 35 percent of teenage boys report they are frequent users.[6] Over 70 percent of young men aged 18–24 regularly visit porn sites each month.[7]

Social media is also becoming a greater problem. A recent poll found that 22 percent of teens log onto their favorite social media site more than 10 times a day. Additionally, over 50 percent of adolescents log onto a social media site more than once a day.[8] You seldom see kids without their nose stuck in their smartphone, texting their friends. The phenomena of *sexting* can cause kids problems for a lifetime, as does the presence of a growing number of sexual predators online. Additionally, constant time online is causing people to lose the ability to communicate effectively and to develop healthy human relationships.

The internet and social networks also provide unrestrained opportunities for bullies to abuse their victims with no accountability. Girls especially seem to be susceptible to cyber-bullying. Their more tender hearts and need for relationship and acceptance make them vulnerable to verbal and written attacks on their character.

Cyber-bullying, in the form of spreading rumors and lies about another through spoken or written words via electronic media, is perhaps more destructive than physical abuse. Kids fear that everyone at school will see them bullied all over cyberspace through social media sites, instant messaging, text messaging, email, blogs, cell phones, or chat rooms. Cyber-bullying is even more potent because it can happen twenty-four hours a day, seven days a week, day or night, and can even find them in the privacy of their own home.

Signs Your Child May Be Being Bullied

- Unexplained injuries.
- Lost or destroyed clothing or other material items.
- Frequent headaches or stomachaches, feeling sick, or faking illness.
- Changes in eating habits like skipping meals or binge eating. Coming home from school hungry because they did not eat lunch.
- Difficulty sleeping or frequent nightmares.
- Declining grades—not wanting to go to school.
- Sudden loss of friends or avoidance of social situations.
- Feelings of helplessness or decreased self-esteem.
- Self-destructive behaviors such as running away from home, harming themselves, or talking about suicide.

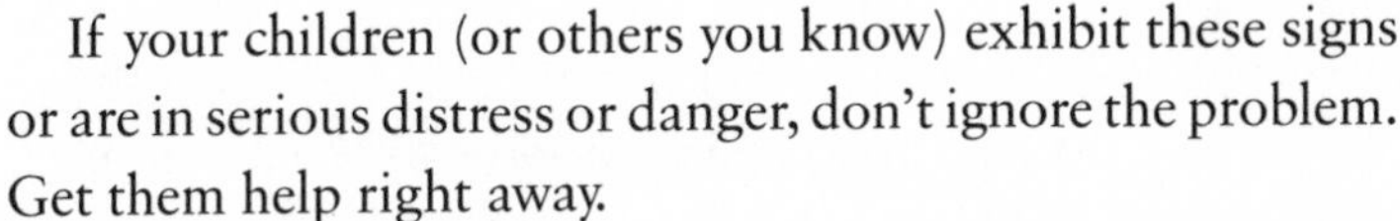

If your children (or others you know) exhibit these signs or are in serious distress or danger, don't ignore the problem. Get them help right away.

Better dads control the type and amount of media to which their children are exposed.

Challenges Faced by Fatherless Boys and Girls

> Any fool . . . can make a baby, but it takes a real man to raise his children.
>
> —Jason "Furious" Styles,
> in *Boyz n the Hood*

Nearly 40 percent of the children in this country now live in a single-parent home. Since 85 percent of single-parent homes are run by moms, that means the majority of those kids are growing up in father-absent homes. Over 42 percent of children being born today are born out of wedlock. Maybe you have children who are not living with you. If so, I encourage you to try to spend as much time as possible with all your children, not just the ones currently living in your home. You matter a lot to all your children, whether they live with you or not.

All children have an innate need for a father's healthy masculine affection. If they receive it, they thrive, but without it they often seek it out in self-destructive ways.

The young people our ministry works with from single-parent homes or other at-risk situations are especially vulnerable. The girls, desperate for affection, so ache for a father's love they willingly accede to the sexual advances of the predatory (and equally fatherless) boys who eagerly take their love before tossing them aside like used tissues. The fatherless boys, wanting so desperately to feel like a man, try to cross the threshold of manhood by sexual conquest of girls, quickly leaving them, as was modeled by the male role models in their lives.

Fatherless kids have a father-sized hole in their souls. The Tempter tries to fill that hole with temptation. Drug dealers, pimps, and hustlers know this—they know fathers matter. Gangs now focus on young boys (eight to nine years old) with no dads. As pastor Mark Strong said during a conference, "A pimp once told me, 'The first question I ask a girl is, Do you have a father? If she says no, I know I got her.'"

Boys and girls from father-absent homes become men and women who suffer the anger, hurt, and pain of fatherlessness. Someone always pays for that pain—usually future generations.

Be a better dad—not just to your kids but to all children. It doesn't take much. But if every man did that, it would fix a lot of problems in the world.

What You Do Matters in Life

Most of us men don't think who we are or what we do makes a difference. We don't think we are all that important. But after reading this book, you already know how important you are in the lives of your wife and children. The truth is, though, you are important to others in ways you never dreamed. Who you are and how you raise your children matters to other people who look to you for encouragement and inspiration. I want to share a few letters I have been fortunate enough to receive over the years. Please know I don't share them to make myself look good; I share them as an example of what God can do when just an average guy steps out and allows himself to be used. Here's an example from a man I met recently:

> *Rick,*
>
> *Having the opportunity to meet you was a blessing and an answer to prayer that I hope I can tell you about someday. I didn't have a chance to let you know the impact you have had on my life, but I want you to know a little bit. Four years ago when my wife and I had our first child, I was lost. I felt inadequate (to say the least) as a man to lead anyone, much more my son. I heard you on the radio, bought your book, and for the first time felt like I could be the father I longed to be (I have read a few more of your books since). I know*

you hear this all of the time and I am very happy I have the chance to also tell you that your legacy includes my family. Your legacy includes the fact that my, now 3, children will grow up with a present father who seeks to lead them in God's purpose and my wife will have a husband who seeks God's will for our family. Thank you, Rick,

SG

Obviously, I am a writer and so I am blessed to have people contact me from time to time who have been impacted by my books or speaking. The truth is, though, as a man and a father, you are being watched by people every day who are trying to see how a man lives his life, makes decisions, solves problems, and raises a family. Fatherless boys are just one example. They are literally almost doomed without a positive male role model to teach them what it means to be a man. This young man attended one of our Single Moms Family Camps with his grandmother, and I gave him a book as a parting gift:

Hello, Mr. Johnson,

I wanted to say thank you for the book "The Power of a Man." This book is amazing! There were so many things I never knew that through your book you taught me. The sad thing is that it does not look like I would ever have been told anything close to what you have written. I have shared your book with friends my age as well as with my youth group who all expressed great interest in reading it. I really loved reading the book and hope my friends will as well. Even though it is not the most comfortable thing to read, it is definitely worth any amount of time to go through and soak up every bit of knowledge.

Gratefully,

BD

Finally, your presence can inspire other fathers and men to do things they might never do if not for your involvement in their life. It's not so much that we as men are special, as much as it is part of the power that God gave us as men and fathers. You have the power, just by virtue of your presence in this world, to make a difference in the lives of people you'll never meet.

Rick,

Just to let you know that your book motivated me to get our company to set up a welding course for young kids in the jungle.

My dad gave me your book, Becoming the Dad Your Daughter Needs, *so I could start figuring out my five-year-old daughter early on. I'm a former MK (missionary kid) of Canadian missionary parents who had worked in South America. I now run the South American operations of a mining exploration company that is mostly staffed at its local levels by a great crew of Christian people from many denominations.*

We are beginning to operate in a very difficult small town in the middle of the jungle that has been the object of small illegal gold mining and cocaine traffic for two decades now on the border of Colombia and Brazil.

One thing I noticed was the miserable conditions of the local youth, especially the girls. Young child prostitution is a great concern here because the place is a confluence of evil forces. Normally it's the mining exploration company that gets the brunt of ill-perceived criticism. But in this town we have drug traffickers, an ironically large police base of 250 young men taken far from their families, some extreme environmentalists that are usually high on narcotics themselves, and local less-than-honest politicians that would shock the rest of the country.

A lot of the native first nations "fathers" are caught in a spiral of alcohol, and as such, they will "sell" their daughters to the men of all these different groups, for the price of another beer.

We haven't started drilling operations yet, but during my trips back and forth to the town, I have had a pain in my heart for the youth. One of the welders in town has been asking us for work. We don't really have an operation started yet, but we do want to help him. So I had just finished your book on the plane as I landed in Bogota, and it gave me an idea.

Next week we are setting up a welding introduction course for 10 boys one day and 10 girls the next day—ages 11–14. My brother heads up Youth for Christ Latin America and he suggests that age group is the key target age.

We never expect these kids to become welders, but something tells me that you are right—the more the girls know about "guy stuff" the less vulnerable some of them will be. The traditional "macho" man of this society is very intimidated by women/girls who would know something about "guy stuff" and the intimidation would be exacerbated if the girl knows more than them about a car engine or a welding technique. Your book struck a chord and we think it might make the girls more confident and less appealing. At least it's a start.

Obviously when we begin our operations, we are going to ramp up the project and try and convince World Vision to come in and be our much more expert social arm.

So just thought you'd find it interesting that your book made it out to the Amazon jungle. (Unfortunately no one else will probably be able to read it because if I leave it out in camp, it WILL get eaten by ants.)

Regards,

AR

He followed up a month later with photos of young girls in the jungle wearing welding gear, working on various projects. How many lives will he change? How many girls will he keep from living lives of hopelessness and despair by being forced to service strange men's sexual lusts? I don't know, but I do know he is compelled to do *something* and that's a whole lot better than just sitting around taking up space and eating groceries.

You don't have to write a book to make a difference in people's lives or to change the world. All you have to do is be present and somewhat intentional in what you do—God can handle the rest. God just wants you as men and fathers to be open and available to be used by him. That can be frightening, but I guarantee it's the most gratifying and satisfying thing you'll ever do. The exhilaration of being scared to death yet soaring with the power of God's wings under you through life making a difference in the lives of others is a joy I pray that you get to experience. God has a mighty plan for your life, but he wants you to step forward in faith in order to fulfill it. Begin today.

You can do it—because you matter!

Wrap-Up

> Warriors are not what you think of as warriors. The warrior is not someone who fights, because no one has the right to take another life. The warrior, for us, is one who sacrifices himself for the good of others. His task is to take care of the elderly, the defenseless, those who cannot provide for themselves, and above all, the children, the future of humanity.
>
> — attributed to Sitting Bull

There is an ancient Jewish tradition that talks about the *Tzadikim Nistarim* (Hebrew) or the "hidden righteous ones" (also called *Lamed Vav Tzadikim*). Mystical Hasidic Judaism as well as other segments of Judaism believe that in every generation there exist thirty-six just and righteous people whose role in life is to justify the purpose of humankind in the eyes of God (*Lamed-vavnik* is the Yiddish term for one of the thirty-six humble righteous ones or Tzadikim mentioned in kabbalah or Jewish mysticism). For the sake of these thirty-six saints, God preserves the world even if the rest of humanity has degenerated to the level of total barbarism. This tradition says that the world is prevented from being submerged in its follies and wickedness by the presence in each generation of a small number of just men who, through their conduct and good deeds, ensure the safety and survival of the people of the world. They are hidden and operate inconspicuously. Nobody knows who they are, they are unknown to each other, and some believe they themselves do not know they are one of the thirty-six.[1]

Whatever the details and origin of this legend (possibly based upon the story of Sodom and Gomorrah), it is a great story with a ring of truth. The world *is* maintained by quite small numbers of ordinary people who, by their presence, with no special claim to merit or distinction, go about their affairs in times of upheaval to provide oases of sanity and continuity. Those who claim to be in control of events strut about in the limelight and manipulate the levers of power without considering the consequences of their actions, many causing considerable damage before being reversed.

I believe these "righteous ones" in the legend may just be good fathers. Anonymous men who dedicate themselves and sacrifice their goals and dreams in order to provide for, nurture, protect, and guide their children and other children. If you are a father, you are quite possibly one of those Tzadikim! You and all the other fathers are the ones who make the world a good and just place. You are the ones who create change in the world. You are the ones whom God looks upon with pride and joy. You are the ones your children need more than any other man on earth. Use your special powers to ensure the safety and survival of those who depend upon you. Without all of you better dads, the world is doomed to fall into despair and hopelessness. With you, there is hope, joy, and goodness.

Welcome to being a Better Dad. May God bless you.

Better Dads Workbook

10 Uncommon Traits
of Exceptional Fathers

Introduction

Hi, Men.

I wanted to create a workbook to go along with this book that would be different than anything I had seen in the marketplace before. I also wanted to create one that a man could go through on his own or with a group of men. But even though you *can* do the things in this workbook on your own, I want to encourage you to find a group of guys to adventure through this with together. As men, we are too isolated. We seldom spend time together with guys unless we are doing something. And from what I can tell, young men today struggle even more finding endeavors that allow social interaction where the proverb of "iron sharpens iron" (Prov. 27:17) can occur.

There are a few requirements that you should be aware of before beginning this study. Each man should agree to all of these conditions before becoming part of the group.

1. **Homework**—Each man should agree to do the homework assigned each week. This is non-negotiable. You will get out of this study what you put into it. Any man who does not do his homework is letting down each of the other members of the group.
2. **Prayer**—Every guy agrees to pray daily for his own family and fellow group members. Additionally, prayer will be part of each week's activities. Nothing draws people closer together than praying together. Each man is strongly encouraged to pray *with* his wife and children as well.
3. **Confidentiality**—Confidentiality is the most important rule. The information shared in the group stays in the group, no matter what. Personal information can't be taken outside the group, even under the pretext of asking someone outside the group to pray for someone else in the group. Married group members should not share with their spouse what other group members have said (unless permission is given). The only exception is if someone reveals that they have done or will do physical harm to another person. At that point the group leader should contact the appropriate authority.

Chapter 1—Have Fun! The Importance of Humor and Play

One quality found in all good families is plenty of laughter in the home. A home with a lot of laughter in it is a healthy home. But happy families do not happen by accident. Here's my question to you: *What is your vision for your family and how are you going to accomplish that vision?*

Laughter releases chemicals that are mentally and physically healthy. A good, hearty belly laugh releases endorphins, the brain's "feel good" chemical. Endorphins allow us to ignore pain and relax. Additionally, laughter releases chemicals (such as serotonin and dopamine) in the body, which produce the feeling of well-being and contentment.

One of your roles as a father is to set the tone of the home for your family. There are times when you will need to be serious and even stern. But I would encourage you to try to promote laughter in your home as often as possible. Here are some thoughts for you and/or your group to think about:

1. Have you sat down with your wife and discussed what you want the tone of your home to be like? If we don't determine what we want, we end up settling for whatever comes along. Write it down, then revisit it every year of so.
2. List five ways you can proactively create laughter in your home. Try to facilitate at least one of them every night after dinner.
3. Tell your kids stories of events that happened to you throughout the day. One of the great joys for children is to sit around Dad's feet and hear him tell stories.

4. Make sure to play with your kids. They need Dad's physicality. Physical play with them develops many areas of their bodies, minds, and psychological development.

Key Tip—Better Dads give lots of physical affection!

Chapter 2—Go Outside Your Comfort Zone: But It's Uncomfortable Out Here!

Engaging with our children on their level in activities *they* like facilitates us bonding deeper with them and allows us to get to know them better. If you aren't willing to go places they want to go and interact with them in their world, you'll never have critical and important conversations with them. They usually won't talk to you about those kinds of things on your level. Especially as they get older. you have to make time for them and intentionally create situations that put you face-to-face with them in their environment. And the best conversations always happen when you are *doing* something together—not when you sit them down for a "talk." This is good news for us dads because as males we can talk better while doing something than we can sitting down across the table face-to-face with someone. We also bond easier by doing things together with another person.

1. Go to your child's school during the day—even if it's just for lunch. What a great surprise for Dad to come by for a visit!
2. Once a month set up a "Dad Night" with each of your children. Take them places they want to go or to a place

where neither of you have ever been before. Discuss with your group something new you learned about your child after each outing.

3. Have you apologized to your children and asked for their forgiveness when you have wronged them? If you make it a habit to do so, it will get easier to do as you go. Share with your group what you did and what happened after you apologized. It's a good way to be held accountable.
4. With your wife, plan and implement at least one EPIC family vacation every year—even if you are too busy or cannot afford it. You can be creative and still make it affordable. Make this a priority—it's important!

Key Tip—Better Dads have the courage to look foolish in front of their kids.

Chapter 3—Surround Yourself with Healthy Friends and Couples: It Matters!

Why is it so difficult for men to make deep, meaningful friendships? Is it because we lack the courage to be vulnerable enough with another man to allow that kind of relationship to develop? Or is it because we are so competitive that we see other men as a challenge instead of an asset. Likely, most men are too insecure (myself included) to allow ourselves to reach out and risk rejection.

But the truth is we need friends in our lives. God created us to need close ties with friends and family. When we lived in clans or tribes, we automatically spent vast amounts of time with groups of men and developed deep, close relationships. It is not only emotionally and psychologically good for us to have friends, but it's physically healthy as well. As I stated earlier, I've never met a good father who lived in a vacuum—who walled himself off from other men. Whether we want to admit it or not, isolation is death to a man. It is the evil one's way of making sure we never become the man and father that God intended us to become. I encourage you to discuss this issue in depth with your small group. Then consider undertaking several of the challenges below.

1. Go out of your comfort zone every day this week and have a meaningful conversation with someone you don't know. Most people never talk to anyone they don't know.
2. Call an old friend you haven't spoken to for a while today. Friendships die when one or both friends fail to initiate contact. Tell your friend you were thinking about them and just wanted them to know you care. Ha! If that doesn't put you outside your comfort zone, nothing will! Do that enough times and you'll start finding it easier to tell people whom you care about that they are important to you.
3. Set up—or encourage your wife to set up—"dates" with other couples. I know—but do it anyway.
4. Encourage your children to have a relationship with your extended family and in-laws. You have to be the one who initiates and facilitates that. It's important.

Key Tip—Better Dads are accountable to other men.

Chapter 4—Communicate with Your Children: *Someone* Is Going to Influence Them

A father's words stay in his children's hearts for the rest of their lives. Some of you men may be either trying to disprove words your father spoke to you ("You're worthless" or "You'll never amount to anything") or are still blessed by words he spoke to you ("I love you" or "I'm so proud of you").

Learning to communicate effectively with your children is one of the greatest tools a Better Dad has at his disposal. Dads who are intentional in using their verbal and written words with their children feel better about the job they are doing, and their children turn out much more happy and well-adjusted. Consider using a few of these strategies to communicate more effectively:

1. Write your children (especially your daughters) notes to put in their lunch bag—or if they don't carry a lunch, text them every day, just so they know you are thinking of them.
2. Challenge yourself to listen to an entire conversation with your children without responding, except to encourage them to continue. At the end, repeat back a condensed version of the conversation so they know you understood them.
3. If you make a mistake or make your child feel bad—apologize. Every time.

Key Tip—Better Dads improve their communication skills because it helps them be successful in all areas of life.

Chapter 5—Develop Your "Brand": When Everyone Knows Your Name

Think of some of the more famous families in the history of the world or even on television. The Cartwrights from the TV show *Bonanza* were known for their integrity, honesty, and loyalty to one another. The Kennedys and Roosevelts were known as political families and the Jacksons as a musical family. The Hatfields and McCoys will be known throughout history as families who couldn't play well together.

What do you want your family to be known as and remembered for? We need to determine which character qualities are most important to us and then be intentional in creating a plan to implement those into our family DNA. Here are some simple things to try to develop your family "brand."

1. Find a college or pro football team you like. Make it your family "team." Get season tickets to the games or pick up tickets for the family whenever possible. If you do get season tickets, make them generational—endowed from one generation to the next. Go to tailgate parties. Wear team clothing and decorate your car on game day. Or watch the games on TV with other like-minded families—make it a game-day party. This develops family traditions that can be passed down from generation to generation. How much fun is that?
2. If you haven't already done so, spend some time brainstorming with your wife (maybe on a getaway weekend) about what three character traits you most want ingrained in your family genetic makeup. These traits are ones that when people mention your family they will

automatically associate them with your family. Now write out a plan to start implementing and teach your children these values on a day-to-day basis. Go over the plan with your children and get their input.

3. Make a pact with your family that you will have dinner together as a family at least five nights a week. This will require sacrifices from all family members in order to be accomplished. Because this is so important to the success of children becoming healthy adults, this is one way a Better Dad leads his family.

Key Tip—Better Dads provide leadership for their family by planning and implementing ways to help each member become more successful in life.

Chapter 6—A Man's Spirituality: Finding Yours So You Can Teach Your Children Theirs

Fathers are an extremely important factor in transmitting faith to their children. Children's perspectives of their earthly father influence their perspective of their heavenly Father. Your children *will* be influenced by their father's faith—or lack thereof. A father who does not believe in anything will have children who will fall for anything. But it's difficult to share something if we don't understand it ourselves. I'm convinced so many men (even Christian men) not only don't understand what they truly believe in their hearts, but don't understand how that confusion impacts the day-to-day decisions they make. When we are lukewarm, tepid, passive, or complacent in our faith, it teaches our children that there are no truths in life and that there is nothing worth getting passionate about in life. It also leaves them without a moral foundation from which to face life.

1. Share the story of your testimony with your children—often. Talk about the challenges you had before coming to Christ and the challenges you've faced since. Tell your children what you believe (know) to be true and why.
2. Discuss with your wife how spiritual warfare may be a factor in some of the challenges your family faces today or has faced in the past.
3. Let your children observe you doing the "mechanics" of faith building: reading the Bible daily, praying daily, praying with your wife, attending church weekly, etc. This teaches them that practice makes perfect.

Key Tip—Better Dads delve within themselves to understand their faith and what they truly believe, no matter how difficult that may be.

Chapter 7—Your Child's Spirituality: Helping Your Children Find Their Way

According to research, fathers are the biggest key to whether children develop a faith system or not. Whether you want the job or not, whether you feel qualified or not—Dad, you *are* the theology professor in your home. You set the spiritual tone and foundation in your home and likely the belief system your children adopt—at least until they are old enough to develop their own, which they will have to eventually. Every day you are teaching your kids about God, faith, truth, and the Bible through your actions and words. Didn't think you were signing up for that when you decided to become a father, did you? And unfortunately for you, once you are in this position, you can't resign. Because even your resignation will teach your kids something about faith. And being passive or apathetic about your spiritual walk teaches them even more.

Consider these and other ways to help your child develop their faith:

1. Help your child understand the principle that whenever we do the right thing for the right reason, we are bound to encounter resistance (spiritual warfare). Often we will feel like we failed in our endeavors. But to do the right thing for the right reason and fail is *not* failure. It is being faithful. And God always rewards faithfulness. Maybe not in the time or way we want, but he always does.
2. Study each of your children. Find out what their strengths and weaknesses are. Then consider what their bent or "way" is—what areas God has gifted them in that they may use to further his kingdom and make a difference in the world. Then brainstorm with your wife ways that you can nurture those gifts to make them bloom within your children.
3. Find activities to do as a family that drive home the importance of ministry work. This might include volunteering at any number of different events or venues.

Or it might be developing your own ministry. Families who work together in ministry bond closely.

Key Tip: Better Dads seek healing for their wounds (especially spiritual ones) so that they can lead their family in healthy spirituality.

Chapter 8—Teaching Character: Allowing Your Children to Suffer

Suffering develops character. Without suffering we never have the opportunity to test ourselves and see what we are made of. If that's true, then it goes without saying that our children need to suffer in order to develop a healthy character. For so many of us the challenge is, how do we allow our children to suffer enough to develop character without traumatizing them? Many parents today "rescue" their kids too often, never allowing them to face the consequences of any of the choices they make. "Helicopter parents" hover over their children, never allowing them to take healthy risks and possibly get hurt. Since it's virtually impossible to succeed at life without taking some risks, these children are psychologically crippled by the very thing their parents think is helping them.

Here are some steps to consider when developing character:

1. Allow your children to fail. Then allow them the privilege of suffering the consequences of their choices. All success comes from failure. We all learn best through our failures, and we develop healthy self-esteem through overcoming failure.

2. Teach your children how to suffer well. Hint: We do that best through example.
3. Make time to talk with your children often about character. Discuss the good character traits of family and friends to illustrate what character looks like. Use the good and bad examples in movie characters to stimulate discussion about why character is necessary in our lives.

Key Tip: Better Dads teach their children to have character by being men of character!

Chapter 9—Children, Members of the Family: Not the Center of the Universe

Your children are gifts from God and should be celebrated as welcome members of the family. But they are not the *center* of the family. Your marriage is the center—the cornerstone—of the family.

Children need firm but loving discipline and guidelines. But it's important to understand the difference between discipline and punishment. How you discipline your children is your business (at least for now), but I don't think any of us fathers want to damage our children; rather, we do want to guide them and instill proper values and manners. With that in mind how do Better Dads ensure that their children are raised properly without trauma but still learn self-discipline? Think about these steps and develop some of your own:

1. Do you have a strategy or plan in place to make sure that you do not discipline your children in anger? Discuss

with your wife what you each think your discipline program should look like. Talk with your children about the need for discipline in their lives and get suggestions on how best to hold them accountable for their actions.

2. Again make sure you and your wife are on the same page regarding the consequences of disciplining your children and what that looks like. Having one parent hold children accountable to one standard while the other parent allows them to get away with that action is not only counterproductive but sends the message that the "inmates run the asylum."
3. Make sure your discipline program is age appropriate. Having the same standards for a seven-year-old and a seventeen-year-old is unfair. Take into consideration each child's maturity level and their personality bent.

Key Tip: Better Dads use discipline that is fair and consistent and realize how destructive their anger can be to young hearts.

Chapter 10—Not in My House: Dad, the Gatekeeper of the Home

Virtually everything our culture promotes involves plundering our home and carrying off our children. Thankfully, one person has the power to offset the world's teaching and influence on their children. That person is Dad.

Whether we want the responsibility or not, as fathers, we *are* the gatekeeper of our home. Mothers might be the decision-makers in the home, but without Dad alongside her to reinforce (and enforce) her decisions, rules might not be as well established and followed. Fathers have an innate authority with children—maybe even a fear factor. Used to an extreme, it is detrimental. But used effectively and responsibly, it serves a good purpose.

Let's look at some ways dads can use their power to offset negative and unhealthy influences in their children's lives:

1. Throughout the time your children are in your home, it is important that you know their friends and be involved in the process of how your children choose those friends. In addition it is vitally important that you know the parents of their friends. With your wife, develop a strategy to monitor and influence the friends your children have and to meet with their parents.
2. Develop a plan on how much media your children are exposed to on a daily basis. If we are not proactive and consistent in this area, too much media exposure (TV, video games, social networking, pornography, etc.) can be extremely damaging to the development of our children.
3. Be a man and father your children respect and look up to. Be involved in making the world a better place. After all, evil prospers when good men do nothing.

Key Tip: Better Dads are present and intentional in protecting their children from harmful influences.

God bless you, men! You are more important than you realize. You matter!

Notes

Chapter 1 Have Fun!

1. Jennifer Welsch and LiveScience, "Why Laughter May Be the Best Pain Medicine," *Scientific American*, September 14, 2011, http://www.scientificamerican.com/article/why-laughter-may-be-the-best-pain-medicine/.

2. Eric Barker, "Six Things the Happiest Families All Have in Common," Barking Up the Wrong Tree, *The Week*, September 3, 2014, http://theweek.com/article/index/266696/6-things-the-happiest-families-all-have-in-common.

Chapter 2 Go Outside Your Comfort Zone

1. Gleaned from Larry Crabb, *Inside Out* (Colorado Springs: NavPress, 2007), 98–99.

2. Jay Payleitner, *10 Conversations Kids Need to Have with Their Dad* (Eugene, OR: Harvest House, 2014), 15.

Chapter 3 Surround Yourself with Healthy Friends and Couples

1. Eric Hoffer, *The True Believer* (New York: Harper & Row, 1951), 40.

2. H. Stephen Glenn and Jane Nelsen, *Raising Self-Reliant Children in a Self-Indulgent World* (Roseville, CA: Prima Publishing, 2000), 16.

3. Joe Kita, *The Father's Guide to the Meaning of Life* (Rodale, Inc. for Hallmark Cards, Inc., 2002), 45.

4. David Murray, "10 Reasons Why Men Have So Much Difficulty Making Friends," *The Christian Post*, April 17, 2014, http://blogs.christianpost.com/guest-views/10-reasons-why-men-have-so-much-difficulty-making-friends-20996/.

5. As cited in Daniel Duane, "Do Men Suck at Friendship?" Mind & Body, *Men's Journal*, May 2014, 58.

6. Ibid.

Chapter 4 Communicate with Your Children

1. Albert Mehrabian, *Silent Messages*, in Blake,"How Much of Communication Is Really Nonverbal?" The Nonverbal Group, August 1, 2014, http://www.nonverbalgroup.com/2011/08/how-much-of-communication-is-really-nonverbal/.

2. Edwin Louis Cole, *Maximized Manhood* (New Kensington, PA: Whitaker House, 2001), 110–13.

3. Glenn and Nelsen, *Raising Self-Reliant Children*, 126.

Chapter 5 Develop Your "Brand"

1. Glenn and Nelsen, *Raising Self-Reliant Children*, 78.

2. Ibid., 79.

3. Brett and Kate McKay, "Fathering with Intentionality: The Importance of Creating a Family Culture," *Art of Manliness* website, July 22, 2013, http://www.artofmanliness.com/2013/07/22/family-culture/.

4. IMDb, John Wayne Quotes, http://m.imdb.com/name/nm0000078/quotes.

5. "Statistics on the Father Absent Crisis in America," Father Facts, *National Fatherhood Initiative*, http://www.fatherhood.org/father-absence-statistics.

6. Gregory Slayton, *Be a Better Dad Today* (Ventura, CA: Regal from Gospel Light, 2012), 74.

Chapter 6 A Man's Spirituality

1. Patrick Morley, *Pastoring Men* (Chicago: Moody, 2009), 41–42.

2. Ibid., 43.

Chapter 7 Your Child's Spirituality

1. Ken R. Canfield, *The 7 Secrets of Effective Fathers* (Wheaton: Tyndale, 1992), 169.

2. Rick I. Johnson, "Is There a Difference in Educational Outcomes in Students from Single Parent Homes?" master's thesis for the degree of Masters in Education (Concordia University Portland, 2009), 31–32.

3. Werner Haug and Phillipe Warner, "The Demographic Characteristics of the Linguistic and Religious Groups in Switzerland," *The Demographic Characteristics of National Minorities in Certain European States*, Vol. 2 of Population Studies No. 31 (Strasbourg: Council of Europe Directorate General III, Social Cohesion, January 2000). Cited in S. Michael Craven, "Fathers: Key to Their Children's Faith," *Christian Post*, June 19, 2011, http://www.christianpost.com/news/fathers-key-to-their-childrens-faith-51331/.

4. Ibid.

5. John Trent and Greg Johnson, *Dad's Everything Book for Sons* (Grand Rapids: Zondervan, 2003), 153.

6. Steven Pressfield, *The War of Art* (New York: Black Irish Entertainment, 2002), 6, 12, 18.

7. Steven Smith and David Marcum, *Catalyst: How Confidence Reacts with Our Strengths to Shape What We Achieve* (Highland, UT: Veracity, 2014), 37.

8. Gleaned from Gary and Joy Lundberg, Familyshare, "Why We Need to Teach Our Children to Pray," http://familyshare.com/why-we-need-to-teach-our-children-to-pray.

Chapter 8 Teaching Character

1. Glenn and Nelsen, *Raising Self-Reliant Children*, 75–76.

2. Dennis Rainey, *Stepping Up: A Call to Courageous Manhood* (Little Rock, AR: Familylife Publishing, 2011), 25.

3. Stephen Mansfield, *Mansfield's Book of Manly Men* (Nashville, TN: Thomas Nelson Publishing, 2013), 157.

Chapter 9 Children, Members of the Family

1. Gleaned from Glenn and Nelsen, *Raising Self-Reliant Children*.

2. Eric Jaffe, "Why Love Literally Hurts," Observer, *Association for Psychological Science*, 26, no. 2, February 2013, http://www.psychologicalscience.org/index.php/publications/observer/2013/february-13/why-love-literally-hurts.html.

3. Gleaned from Glenn and Nelsen, *Raising Self-Reliant Children*.

4. Richard Lavoie, "When the Poker Chips Are Down," YouTube, August 26, 2013, http://www.youtube.com/watch?v=Vsl_XiyJupg.

5. Guest post by Edie of Life in Grace, *Living Well Spending Less*, "Five Tips for Raising Kids you Actually Like," June 1, 2014, http://www.livingwellspendingless.com/2011/06/01/5-tips-for-raising-children-you-like-edie-lifeingrace/, in Ruth Soukup.

6. David Sper, "How Can a Parent Find Peace of Mind?" Discovery Series (Grand Rapids: RBC Ministries, 1991 & 2001), 10–11.

7. Gleaned from Glenn and Nelsen, *Raising Self-Reliant Children*.

8. Adapted from Proverbs 13:24.

9. Brett & Kay McKay, "Why You Should Parent Like a Video Game," *Art of Manliness* blog site, http://www.artofmanliness.com/2014/08/19/why-you-should-parent-like-a-video-game/.

10. Glenn and Nelsen, *Raising Self-Reliant Children*, 145.

11. Gwen Dewar, "ADHD in Children: Are Millions Being Unnecessarily Medicated?" *Parenting Science*, last modified March 2013, http://www.parentingscience.com/ADHD-in-children.html.

Chapter 10 Not in My House

1. "Sandbar Fight," *Wikipedia*, http://en.wikipedia.org/wiki/Sandbar_Fight. The *Wikipedia* author combined eyewitnesses accounts "to weave a consistent narrative," from which this excerpt is drawn.

2. Glenn and Nelsen, *Raising Self-Reliant Children*, vii.

3. Robin Yapp, "Children Who Watch Too Much TV May Have 'Damaged Brain Strictures,'" Health, *Daily Mail Online*, January 10, 2014, http://www.dailymail.co.uk/health/article-2537240/Children-watch-TV-damaged-brain-structures.html.

4. Sunory Dutt, "Beware the Negative Effects of Too Much Screen Time for Children," Life section, *South China Morning Post*, May 19, 2014, http://www.scmp.com/lifestyle/health/article/1513555/beware-negative-effects-too-much-screen-time-children.

5. "Too Much Time Online," BEaPRO Balance, *iKeepSafe*, http://www.ikeepsafe.org/be-a-pro/balance/too-much-time-online/.

6. Luke Gilbertson, "Get the Latest Pornography Statistics," *Covenant Eyes*, February 19, 2013, http://www.covenanteyes.com/2013/02/19/pornography-statistics/.

7. "The Stats on Internet Pornography," *Tech Addiction*, July 8, 2014, http://www.techaddiction.ca/files/porn-addiction-statistics.jpg.

8. Anna Norat, "Kids & Social Media," *Pediatric Health Care Alliance*, http://www.pedialliance.com/socialmediaguide.

Wrap-Up

1. Wikipedia, "Tzadikim Nistarim," http://en.wikipedia.org/wiki/Tzadikim_Nistarim, accessed July 21, 2014.

Rick Johnson is a bestselling author of *That's My Son*; *That's My Teenage Son*; *That's My Girl*; *Better Dads, Stronger Sons*; and *Becoming Your Spouse's Better Half*. He is the founder of Better Dads and is a sought-after speaker at many large parenting and marriage conferences across the United States and Canada. Rick, his wife, Suzanne, and their grown children live in Oregon. To find out more about Rick Johnson, visit www.betterdads.net.

Join Rick and other Fathers on the Better Dads Movement

I am seeing more and more men of all ages who want to be better men and fathers. Many come up to me after I speak and want to know if I have a program that will go deeper and help them become the kind of men and fathers they want to be. They are desperate and don't know where to turn. The good news is that now we do have just the program they've been looking for.

At Better Dads, we want you to know one thing, and that is, You Matter. No matter where you are or what you have done, there is still time to become a Better Dad. No matter how old or how young your children are or even if you are yet to be a father, we want to walk with you in your fatherhood experience. We want you to know that we believe in you and that you are not alone.

We invite you to join us on our mission to see a world filled with Better Dads through our Fathers Mentoring Fathers experience. To learn more about this, go to http://betterdads.net/father-mentoring.

Join the Better Dads movement where Better Dads equal Better Families and . . . this equals a Better World!

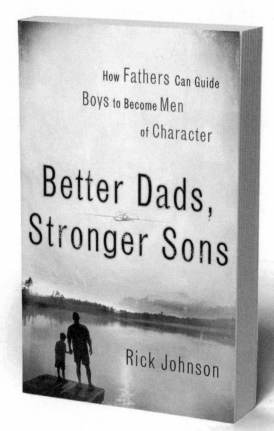

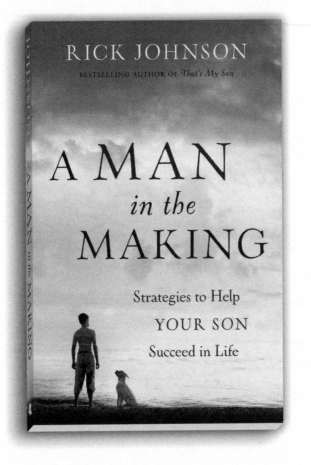